HEALTHY PRAYER

Integrating Structure, Silence, and Spontaneity

RYAN POST

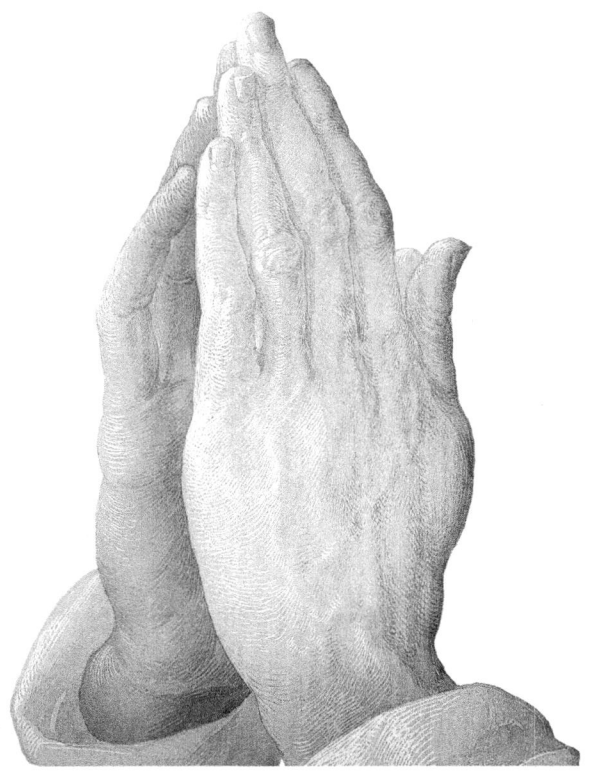

Follow Ryan's personal blog at www.ryanpost.life and visit www.healthyprayer.com to read more articles from Ryan Post on prayer.

Healthy Prayer: Integrating Structure, Silence, and Spontaneity
Copyright © 2018 by Ryan Post
All rights reserved.
ISBN: 978-1-949709-11-7

Cover Design: Jim LePage www.jimlepage.com
Editing: Ellen Edelman

Unless otherwise specified, all scripture is taken from The Holy Bible, English Standard Version (ESV), copyright © 2001 by Crossway Bibles, a division of Good News Publishers. Used by permission. All rights reserved.

*For Carson and Reagan
with deep love and gratitude*

CONTENTS

Author's Note ix
Preface... xi

Chapter One – The Fruit of Healthy Prayer 1
Chapter Two – Playing Jazz Piano 15
Chapter Three – Granddaddy's Recliner 33
Chapter Four – Pigs in a Blanket............................. 45
Chapter Five – Morning Prayer Trellis 63
Afterword 87

Appendix I – Morning Prayer Trellis (Simplified) ... 93
Appendix II – "Prayer for The Week" Guide......... 103
Appendix II – The Lord's Prayer As A Trellis 125
Acknowledgements.. 131

AUTHOR'S NOTE

At the end of each chapter, I have included several questions for group discussion. If this book is being used in the context of a small group, I recommend meeting once a week for four weeks (Chapters 1-4). After the fourth meeting, I recommend taking three weeks off to give time for each person in the group to use the "prayer trellis" I describe in Chapter 5. I would suggest meeting again after three weeks or so to discuss the questions given after Chapter 5.

PREFACE

Writing a book was never really a goal of mine. Vocationally, I have always self-identified as preacher first, content to read what other people have written.

But three years into pastoring my church in South Louisiana, I experienced a dynamic shift in my prayer life. I discovered an approach to prayer that was a bit foreign to me, but once I experienced it I couldn't get enough. This shift in prayer set me on a course that began to slowly transform my marriage, my parenting, and my approach to life and ministry.

Not long after, I decided to begin teaching the people in my church what I was discovering about prayer. Every couple months or so, I began hosting "prayer workshops" in my living room. I would take 8-12 people at a time and teach about prayer for three hours on a Saturday morning.

As people have attended these prayer workshops, it has been so encouraging to hear stories from many who have experienced a similar transformation in their own prayer lives. As word began to spread, other pastors and leaders from around my region began inviting me to come share with their people what I've been learning about prayer. Teaching about prayer has become my favorite thing I do as a pastor.

One of my goals in writing *Healthy Prayer* is to inspire you to come to a place where you are more consistently and passionately coming to God in prayer. I really believe my most fundamental task as a pastor is to equip people to come to God on their own—to cultivate a first-hand spirituality.

One reason I am so passionate about this is because I believe that most Christians struggle with prayer. If we were to take a scientific poll of weekly church-attendees and find out what percentage of them spend at least ten minutes a day in focused prayer, I'm inclined to believe the number would be alarmingly low.

Obviously, this alone is an issue of concern. But let's dig a little deeper. Why is it that people pray so little? There may be many reasons, of course. As one who has spent much time providing spiritual counsel to others, it is my observation that we frequently bring wrong expectations to prayer. Prayer is often seen as a way to get God to do what we think he ought to do. And when that doesn't seem to happen as consistently as we'd like, we become frustrated and perhaps a bit disillusioned with prayer itself.

One of the most compelling requests made throughout the Biblical narrative comes from one of the twelve disciples. *"Lord, teach us to pray."* These are men who had been around prayer their entire lives. Presumably, at least some of them had been attending synagogue weekly since childhood. Prayer was not an unfamiliar concept to them. But they knew on some intuitive level that something was missing. And they had enough courage and desire to lean forward and ask the question—"Will you teach us?"

My only request of you as a reader is to approach this book from a place of spiritual hunger. And I don't think it's a stretch for me to assume that the very fact you're reading this book right now is because on some level you crave something more.

I certainly don't claim to be some sort of prayer guru. But by the grace of God and through the help of others, I've been able to tap into some truths about prayer that I cannot help but share with as many people as I can.

I know what it's like to struggle with prayer. I know what it's like to feel as if I'm praying in circles, never getting anywhere. But I have also learned what prayer is like when it is approached in a healthy way.

Throughout this book I will be sharing about the beauty of integrating the elements of structure, silence, and spontaneity into your prayer life. This approach is nothing new. It's as old as prayer itself.

Perhaps one or more of these elements may be unfamiliar to your prayer life. But I have come to believe that all three of them are essential to healthy prayer.

So I invite you to join me on what I hope will be an amazing journey with God that will slowly and organically begin to transform every aspect of your life.

CHAPTER ONE
THE FRUIT OF HEALTHY PRAYER

"³⁷ And he said to him, 'You shall love the Lord your God with all your heart and with all your soul and with all your mind. ³⁸ This is the great and first commandment. ³⁹ And a second is like it: You shall love your neighbor as yourself.'" (Matthew 22:37-39)

I can still remember the name of the preacher. I can still remember the message he preached. I can still remember the drama piece that was used at the end of his message. Because that night, at a youth rally in Des Allemands, Louisiana, I had my first pivotal encounter with Jesus.

I was an awkward, tall, skinny thirteen-year-old struggling with the turbulent waters of teenage angst and depression. I had been raised in a church environment my entire life. But until then, Jesus was just a person from long ago who did a bunch of cool things. He was a flannel-graph figure. I needed something more substantial.

That night, for the first time, Jesus became a living reality. After the preacher finished his message, I knelt down at the altar, and with tears streaming down my face, I committed my life to Jesus. It was (and still is) the most important moment of my life.

Instantly, the course of my life took a dramatic turn. Gone were all of my middle-school fantasies of one day throwing passes in the NFL or playing guitar for a famous grunge-rock band. From that point on, my singular focus was to passionately serve Jesus with the hope and expectation of eventually entering into vocational ministry.

Today, I can reminisce through those teenage years with a smile on my face. They were volatile years filled with spiritual peaks and valleys. I can recall one particular year when I came back from church camp on such a spiritual high, I "borrowed" several stacks of evangelistic tracts from a closet in my church and started handing them out at school. When they were all gone, I simply designed and printed my own, stamping the church address on the back (without the pastor's permission, of course).

One area of particular interest to me early on was prayer. I remember having an intense desire for prayer.

I think anyone who has ever had a meaningful encounter with God can relate to that desire. And thankfully, I grew up in a church where I was taught the importance of having a daily, consistent prayer life.

The trouble is, throughout my younger life, I cannot remember anyone ever actually teaching me how to pray. The only advice I can ever really remember receiving is the ever-popular, "*Well, just talk to God. That's all prayer is. Be yourself, and talk to him.*"

Which sounds like great advice. But it is built on the misguided assumption that prayer is merely expressing oneself—which inevitably leads to selfish prayer.

This is exactly the way I would describe the early stages of my prayer journey. And the more conscious I was of my selfishness, the more I tried to "fix" my prayer life by saying things I thought God wanted to hear. Which was inauthentic. And the more conscious I was of my inauthenticity, the more frustrated I became. And the more frustrated I became, the less frequently I attempted to pray.

Part of the problem was my motive for prayer. Earlier in my spiritual journey, during my teenage years, I can remember setting a goal for myself – thirty minutes of prayer every day. Thirty minutes seemed like a nice, round number. It was the length of an episode of *Saved by the Bell*. It seemed quite attainable.

For the first few days, I figured things were going pretty well. I was enjoying my time of prayer each day, and I was especially satisfied by the realization that I had made a goal and was sticking to it.

However, after a few days, I recognized a strange dynamic at play. I came to grips with the awareness that my motivation wasn't so much about making meaningful connection with God as much as it was about the feeling of gratification I received after achieving my measurable goal.

It was as though I had a mental image of God watching over me with a checklist: "Make sure you pray a full thirty minutes today – if you do, I'll put another star on your refrigerator chart!"

The actual content of my prayer life was secondary. What was prioritized was a feeling of "right-ness" produced by my own self-generated effort. This is a clear example of wrong thinking about prayer.

The primary purpose of prayer is not to manipulate God to do what we think he should do. It is not to earn brownie points with God. Nor is it to produce in us a certain feeling of "right-ness." *The primary purpose of prayer is to be properly formed.*

> *"Prayer is the central avenue God uses to transform us." – Richard Foster*

If the aim of kingdom living is about loving God and loving people, then prayer only exists to serve that purpose. In other words, prayer only has value insofar as it helps form us into self-sacrificial, kingdom-minded, others-oriented people.

Put simply, loving well is the fundamental task of a kingdom person. And healthy prayer can help form us into people who love well…not in a contrived way, but naturally. Organically.

> *"Special experiences, faithfulness to the church, correct doctrine, and external conformity to the teachings of Jesus all come along … more or less automatically, when the inner self is transformed. But they do not produce such a transformation. The human heart must be plowed much more deeply." – Dallas Willard*

Healthy prayer is one of the most essential ways that

this "plowing" takes place as we learn how to properly position ourselves under the hand of the Holy Spirit.

Healthy prayer is to the Christian life what an exercise regimen is to a marathon runner. Commitment to a well-formed exercise regimen over time can empower a person to do what she cannot do based on desire alone. Mere desire is not enough to complete a marathon. Desire must be funneled through a well-formed regimen.

Similarly, we may *desire* to be the kind of people who naturally love our enemies, forgive our transgressors, and bless our persecutors, but without funneling our desire through a wise, well-formed prayer "regimen," we will become well-acquainted with failure. And over time, repeated failures can lead to a loss of hope and an unwillingness to even engage in the attempt.

So while prayer is not the "end-all, be-all," it is a critical, indispensable means by which the Holy Spirit can form our character, empowering us to walk in obedience to the will of Christ.

> *"Prayer is the ultimate empowerment of the people of God." - Richard Rohr*

Through healthy prayer, we can be shaped into the kind of people who remain calm and at peace in the face of betrayal. The kind of people who respond to crises with uncommon wisdom rather than react with unbridled emotion. The kind of people who have the power to forgive our enemies. The kind of people who are content to serve in obscurity rather than anxiously grasp for attention.

This is the fruit of the abundant life Jesus wants to cultivate in us. But we cannot skim our way into this kind of life.

Nor can we manufacture this fruit on our own. Jesus said, "If you remain in me and I in you, you will bear much fruit; *apart from me you can do nothing*" (John 15:5).

These things only happen through *healthy* prayer infused by the Spirit of God. If prayer is simply a means of "expressing ourselves" to God, we get nowhere. We go round-and-round in circles. Even if we are filled with all the passion in the world, we are like a steam locomotive without a track.

Healthy prayer is a basic combination of spiritual passion (steam) with a well-designed prayer structure (track). If we have one without the other, we will remain stranded with no way to advance. At best, we will sputter along in frustration and eventually depletion.

But combined together, we now have a way forward. With steady engagement, we will progressively become passionate about the things God is passionate about. We will begin to desire what God desires. We will begin to feel the way God feels about things. We will begin to see things from God's perspective.

THE MUSCADINE TRELLIS

Somehow I managed to live the first 35 years of my life having never heard of the sweet nectar of heaven that is the muscadine grape. One summer evening a couple in our church welcomed my wife (Carrie) and me over to their house for dinner. Soon after we arrived, the husband invited me to taste some grapes from the vine in their backyard.

I had eaten grapes plenty of times throughout my life — the ordinary kind in the produce section of a typical grocery store. But I had never tasted a muscadine before. I'm not sure I had ever even heard the word.

That August evening in my friends' backyard when I squeezed the juice of that first grape into my mouth, my life was changed forever. I'm pretty sure I actually said it out loud: "Where have you been all my life?"

After dinner, our friends sent me home with a gallon-size plastic bag full of muscadines.

They were all gone by the next day.

Within a few days I was already researching information on how to plant a vine of my own in my backyard. I was confident I could talk Carrie into the idea. I wasn't worried about *that*.

What I *was* worried about was my terrible track record with gardening. Over the years I have made several attempts to plant gardens in my yard. The results have been nothing short of embarrassing. I can kill a plant almost overnight.

Nevertheless, the risk versus reward disparity was overwhelming. So early February, I formulated my plan and began to put it into action.

The first step was to build my trellis. This involved digging holes, planting poles, and stretching wire. But after a few hours of work (and a couple trips to the hardware store), I was ready to plant my vine.

The purpose of the trellis is rather simple. The trellis is the support structure for the vine. It gives the vine something to which it can cling. It enables the vine to ascend, training the vine according to a prescribed path in order to position it for maximum fruitfulness.

Without the trellis, the vine would scarcely have a chance. It would awkwardly tilt and lurch over the ground, searching blindly for something, anything to which it could fasten itself. Fruit would be minimal, if any at all.

For much of my life, this described my prayer life. While I wouldn't say the early stages of my prayer journey were entirely fruitless, I always intuitively knew that something was amiss. I felt like a vine sprawled out on the ground, desperate for something to which I could cling.

What I needed was a trellis. A certain degree of structure. Not to restrict me or to stifle my growth. But to do the exact opposite. To train the orientation of my heart and mind heavenward, guiding me towards a trajectory that could enable my life to flourish with the fruitfulness of Christ-like character.

Throughout this book I will be describing some of the key components to building a "prayer trellis" that can pull one out of a self-centered, self-dependent mode of prayer and provide a healthy, Christ-centered, and Spirit-led movement of prayer that will bring transformation from the inside-out.

I have personally experienced the joy of healthy, formative prayer. What used to be a frustrating and inconsistent aspect of my spirituality has become a vibrant, life-giving practice that is gradually, incrementally changing my life. I have never been hungrier for prayer. It is the highlight of my day, each and every day.

So I want to show you a more fruitful way to pray—whether you're somewhat new to prayer, or whether you're a prayer veteran.

Like planting a new vine, it will demand a lot of work. It will take a lot of time. It will require you to trust the process.

But in order to live fruitful lives we must enter into the slow, steady process of healthy, formative prayer that is infused by the Spirit of God. It is a process that cannot be hurried or rushed. It is a process that will take a lifetime.

Yet if we are willing to be carefully rooted, nurtured, and pruned in healthy prayer, fruit will be sure to follow.

DISCUSSION QUESTIONS

CHAPTER ONE

1. What has your experience with prayer been like thus far in your life? If you were to use one or two words to describe your prayer life right now, what would you say?

2. Describe your first memorable encounter with God. What was it like? How did it affect you in the days and weeks that followed?

3. What has been one of the most significant challenges you've encountered in your prayer life?

4. If the primary purpose of prayer is to be properly formed, what is one particular area of your life that you recognize needs some healthy formation?

CHAPTER TWO

PLAYING JAZZ PIANO

"Lord, teach us to pray." (Luke 11:1b)

My fascination with music began developing at a very young age. I sang in church for the first time before I was in kindergarten. Throughout my childhood I learned to play several musical instruments, and I began writing songs in my early teenage years.

By far, my favorite instrument to play is the piano. I took piano lessons for a year with my Aunt Danelle when I was six years old. When I sat on the bench to perform at my first recital, my feet couldn't even reach the pedals.

Aunt Danelle taught me some basic chords, scales, and music theory that would serve as my foundation. Over the next several years, through many hours of practice I began to learn how to improvise fairly proficiently.

The reason I love the piano so much is because once you learn the basic structure of the chords, scales, and progressions, it is one of the most enjoyable instruments to play. Unlike the guitar, a piano won't cause calluses to develop on your fingertips, and in my opinion, the piano allows for more creative expression than most other instruments.

Perhaps it's because I am originally from the New Orleans area, but I have always enjoyed hearing jazz piano. Whether it is the free-wheeling style of Herbie Hancock or the classic French Quarter sounds of Dr. John, jazz piano just resonates with me. I have always appreciated the years of practice that is required to become a proficient jazz pianist capable of improvising an amazing solo.

Take a jazz virtuoso like Vince Guaraldi for example. You may not recognize that name, but you're almost certainly familiar with his music. If you have ever seen a *Peanuts* cartoon with Charlie Brown, you've heard some of Guaraldi's famous piano compositions.

When Guaraldi would perform on stage, his musicianship looked effortless. It was almost as if he barely had to think about what he was doing. Of course, his piano work was quite sophisticated, but he made it look easy.

However, what enabled Guaraldi to improvise so proficiently was the fact that early on, before he ever became a successful musician, he had to embrace the structure of jazz piano. He had to learn specific scales, chord structures, and progressions that are unique to jazz music.

Every single day as a young boy, Guaraldi had to sit at his piano and memorize those scales and patterns. He had to play them over and over again. I imagine this daily routine might have been tedious at times.

However, as Guaraldi continued to embrace the structure of these chords and progressions on a daily basis, this practice was building a solid foundation for his musical future. Eventually he internalized these scales and patterns so well that over time, they became engrained into his memory.

After some time when he looked at a set of piano keys, he began to see it through the lens of a jazz pianist. It was because of his mastery of the structure that he was now free to explore the world of jazz improvisation.

See, you can have all the raw, musical talent in the world and have a deep desire to one day become a great musician. And you may even be able to figure out a few elements on your own. But until you are willing to commit yourself to learning some level of musical structure, you will never be able to play an instrument as masterfully as someone like Vince Guaraldi or Herbie Hancock or Dr. John. It is the structure underneath that harnesses one's musical talent and provides a launching pad for a pianist to be able to improvise skillfully.

No matter how much musical potential a person may have, it never automatically translates to the mastery of a musical instrument. Of course talent, passion, and interest are all essential, but the reality is that from the very beginning every great musician must also embrace structure.

What on earth does this have to do with prayer? It has *everything* to do with prayer. I have discovered that one of the most important things we can do with our prayer lives is to embrace some degree of structure. Otherwise, the locomotive has no track. The vine has no trellis.

I have heard this same story over and over again throughout my life. An enthusiastic believer seeks advice on how to pray. The response is simply, "Well, just talk to God." Indeed, this is advice I can remember receiving early in my walk with Christ. But I have found this to be an unhelpful response.

It is a bit like putting someone in front of a piano who has never touched one before and saying, "Here. Play a piano solo like Ray Charles." It's going to sound sloppy. It's going to be hard to listen to.

The problem, of course, is not with God. It is with us. Without any sense of structure, we tend to pray out of our*selves*. And when we pray out of our*selves* the inevitable result is we tend to pray *sel*fishly. We have no choice. Before long, we get frustrated and either give up for a period of time, or we plow forward out of sheer devotion but never really progress beyond a certain level.

No matter how much steam a locomotive has, without a track it never really gets anywhere. The same is true with prayer. Even if we are full of passion and enthusiasm, if transformation is going to happen we need the help of a well-crafted, theologically-rich, time-tested prayer structure.

We are a vine that needs a trellis that can train the orientation of our hearts and minds heavenward, guiding us towards a trajectory that will enable our lives to flourish with the fruitfulness of Christ-like character.

EMBRACING STRUCTURE

For the first 22 years of my committed Christian life, my prayer life was sporadic and unsatisfying. I had always been taught the necessity of consistent, daily prayer and certainly tried with best intentions to maintain that standard. However, so often I encountered a variety of problems.

There were often days and times when I intended to pray but felt like I had no idea where to start. My intentions were pure, but the conversation was forced and awkward. I also had experiences in which I would pour out my heart to God, sharing intense burdens with him. And yet, it felt like part of me was either attempting to manipulate God or treat him as some type of divine therapist who merely listens to my gripes.

That isn't to say that my feeble attempts at prayer were in any way unproductive or ignored by God. God is often more patient and merciful towards us than we realize. But I always intuitively knew that *there must be a better way to do this.*

By my mid-30s, while pastoring a local church, I reached a breaking point. The mounting pressure of my duties as a pastor was beginning to force me to re-evaluate my spiritual health. Out of desperation, I did something I had never done up until that point. I went on a 24-hour retreat at a campground nearby to meet with God. It was during that time that I made a pivotal decision.

I told myself, *"Out of all the things I do as a lead pastor (preaching, teaching, counseling, leading a staff, overseeing finances, etc.), if there is one thing that I want to learn how to do really, really well, it is prayer."*

So over the course of a year-and-a-half, healthy prayer became a focused pursuit of mine. I immersed myself in the subject, reading stacks of books written by a wide range of authors, listening to numerous podcasts and sermons on the subject, and attending prayer events.

On this journey, one of the greatest breakthroughs I received came through the embrace of structure. What is an example of the kind of "structure" I am referring to?

For a simple, well-known example, let's consider the Lord's Prayer. When the disciples asked Jesus, "Lord, teach us to pray," Jesus didn't tell them, "Just talk to God." He gave them a prayer. "When you pray, *say…*"

Now, you can use the Lord's Prayer in all kinds of ways. For example, I frequently teach people how to use it as an outline for prayer. I find that to be a very helpful practice. But it is also perfectly fine to use it as it was originally given and as it was originally used – as a complete prayer.

I know some Evangelicals, Pentecostals, and Charismatics may get a little nervous about the idea of using the Lord's Prayer as a complete prayer, particularly if they have some background in a more liturgical tradition. But not only is the Lord's Prayer taken directly from scripture, it is a prayer given to us by *the Lord himself*. What could be unhealthy about using the prayer given to us by Jesus himself?

Now, we certainly shouldn't pray the Lord's Prayer casually or thoughtlessly. I do understand that people can sometimes take the Lord's Prayer and turn it into a meaningless recitation of words. This form of prayer has no value.

Yet the truth is, we can also be guilty of the same thing even in improvised prayer. I can't tell you how many times I have caught myself in prayer speaking to God absent-mindedly, without any reflection upon the words I was offering to him. The value is not found in the actual words. The value is in the heart behind the words.

But with the help of the Holy Spirit, and when done with careful thought and reflection, words can be used to form our hearts.

The simple purpose of the Lord's Prayer is to serve as a trellis. The trellis is not meant to give life to the vine. The trellis is only there to support the vine and give it something to cling to. The life is found in the vine itself. So any criticism that structured prayer is "dead" is a misunderstanding of its purpose. What is either alive or dead is the person praying.

However, if you can combine a spiritually alive person with a solid prayer structure, eventually something beautiful will emerge.

So I have found great value in adding structure to my prayer life. Now, to be clear, the use of structure does not preclude the use of "improvised prayer." I always include time for improvised prayer every single day, just as I always have. It's just that now, I'm buttressing it with healthy structure.

For example, before I rush to offer my own words to God, I take several minutes praying through Psalm 23, sections of Psalm 91 and Psalm 103, the Lord's Prayer, and other elements. Therefore, when I do begin to offer my own spontaneous words to God, my heart and mind have already been conditioned and prepared in a life-giving way. Thus, my own improvised prayer will inevitably take on a healthier and less selfish quality. To put it differently, the piano solo is going to sound a little bit more like Vince Guaraldi.

Much of the morning prayer structure I use every day (which can be found in Chapter 5) comes directly from Scripture. Praying through Scripture has been an ongoing practice of God's people for at least 3,000 years.

But I have also enjoyed using written prayers that have been handed down to me by the body of Christ. These are well-written, biblically-sound prayers that have stood the test of time. For example, the following prayer is attributed to Francis of Assisi:

> *Lord, make me an instrument of your peace;*
> *where there is hatred, let me sow love;*
> *where there is injury, pardon;*
> *where there is doubt, faith;*
> *where there is despair, hope;*
> *where there is darkness, light;*
> *where there is sadness, joy.*
> *O Divine Master,*

grant that I may not so much seek to be consoled,
as to console;
to be understood, as to understand;
to be loved, as to love.
For it is in giving that we receive,
it is in pardoning that we are pardoned,
and it is in dying that we are born to eternal life.
Amen.

What a beautiful, powerful prayer! I include this in my prayer time every morning. And as I slowly move through it, the Holy Spirit is at work. Every so often, there may be a certain phrase or word that he puts his finger on that carries special meaning or application for that particular moment.

So this is anything but mindless, heartless repetition. Whether I am praying through a scriptural passage like Psalm 23 or using a beautiful prayer like the Prayer of Francis, I am doing so with deep thought and reflection as I engage in partnership with the Holy Spirit.

Here's another example. Pete Scazzero, in his book *The Emotionally Healthy Leader*, offers a wonderful prayer to pray over one's spouse:

Lord, grant me the strength to answer your call to be a living sign of your love. Make my love for _____ to be like your love for him/her. Passionate, permanent, intimate, unconditional, and life-giving. May I be as present to _____ as you are to him/her, so that all the world can see your presence manifested in our tender love for one another. Help us both to stay close to you in the body of Christ, and continue to nourish our love with your love. In Jesus' name, Amen.

To be transparent, I have, at times, been a rather selfish husband. I have often made a bad habit of getting home from the office and taking a long, extended siesta in my recliner, leaving my wife to take care of almost all of the household duties.

After reading this prayer in Scazzero's book, I was inspired to begin using it in my morning prayer time. It has had a profound impact on my marriage. I cannot pray a sentence like "May I be as present to Carrie as you are to her" with any degree of integrity unless I am willing to allow it to shape the way I think and act. And as my wife will testify, the result is that I am now far more involved in everyday household duties than I have ever been before. Not because of external pressure, but because of the internal work of the Holy Spirit through a healthy, Christ-centered prayer.

This is how the addition of some degree of structure in prayer can gradually, incrementally transform our lives.

Now again, no matter how much structure we use in prayer, it is also vital that we offer our own words to God as well. Any good husband worth his salt won't just simply sign his name to his wife's Valentine's Day card. He will personalize it with his own words.

But when we offer our own words to God, we must take our time, choosing our words carefully. We must be authentic before him.

PRAYER AND IMPRESSION MANAGEMENT

One of the common anxieties we tend to share with one another is the concern for the opinions of others. And the primary tool we use to shape their opinions is our speech. Whether consciously or not, much of our speech is filtered through the intent of manipulating the impression others have of us. We surmise that through the craftiness of our words, we can leave people with the impression that we are better, smarter, or holier than we actually are. Therefore, often without thinking, our choice of words flows out of an intent to manipulate and control.

This is often the source of our impulse to pray with constant speech. At least on some level, perhaps there is some engrained notion deep in the recesses of one's mind that "if I can just say the right things, I can manage God's impression of me (or at least my own self-impression)." Of course we may never acknowledge or even take time to reflect and observe this reality, but I suspect this to be a huge factor that fuels the wordiness of prayer for many people.

The solution must be applied carefully and deliberately. Our compulsion to speak must be met with the discipline of careful pauses. We must train our minds to acknowledge each and every time we pray that God sees truth and knows truth. He cannot be deceived or manipulated. When God sees you, he doesn't have a "perspective," an "opinion," or an "impression." He sees you exactly as you are. Even the parts of yourself that remain hidden to you lie open and bare in his sight.

Therefore, there is no need to attempt to "impress" God with the length of your prayer, the volume of your speech, or the quality and speed of your vocabulary. Any attempt to use speech to manage God's "impression" of you is futile, and it becomes a significant barrier to healthy, formative prayer.

The primary purpose of prayer is to be properly formed. This process can only begin to move forward when there is a commitment to being truthful and genuine. This is the foundation of every healthy relationship.

Therefore, the goal of prayer is not simply to learn how to say the right thing at the right time but to always be truthful and real, recognizing that the "Spirit of truth" is at work even when his movement is imperceptible.

So resist the impulse to kick into autopilot. Empty, meaningless speech may sound proper and pious, but without passion and conviction, it profits nothing.

> *"Be not rash with your mouth, nor let your heart be hasty to utter a word before God, for God is in heaven, and you are on earth. Therefore let your words be few" (Ecclesiastes 5:2).*

By contrast, it is much more helpful and meaningful to be deliberate and reflective with the words you employ in prayer. Develop the use of periodic pauses between key thoughts and sentences.

Speak meaningfully. Speak deliberately. Make it a goal to give substantial reflection to every sentence you offer to God in prayer. This doesn't mean your prayer cannot be conversational in pace and tone. But it should be purposeful and flow out of your heart. A couple sentences of authentic, carefully-chosen words are much more profitable than a lengthy, continuous stream of mindless, empty babble.

DISCUSSION QUESTIONS
CHAPTER TWO

1. Describe your current prayer patterns. How often do you pray? When you take time for focused prayer, do you have a certain model you follow? What areas do you pray about?

2. What has been your experience with using structure in your prayer life?

3. Of all the illustrations used thus far (muscadine trellis, jazz pianist, and steam locomotive), which one resonates with you the most? Why?

4. Can you identify any examples of bad prayer habits you've observed (whether in your own life or in someone else's)?

CHAPTER THREE
GRANDDADDY'S RECLINER

"You are my son, whom I love; with you I am well pleased." (Luke 3:22b, NIV)

My grandfather, Joe Broach, was a man of calm, quiet strength. I can still remember being a small boy sitting in his lap in his living room recliner, watching football on Sunday afternoons. "Granddaddy" was the kind of man you could sit in a room with for two or three hours, perfectly content without speaking a single word. There was something comforting and peaceful about simply being with Granddaddy. Even after all these years, I have distinct memories of just sitting with Granddaddy on a quiet, tranquil afternoon.

I suppose most of us have a person like that in our lives. The kind of person you can go on a long road trip with and not feel the pressure to sustain constant conversation. Granddaddy was like that. If he had something to say, he would say it. But he was quite comfortable with silence.

To this day, I cannot specifically remember anything he ever said to me. But I do remember what it was like to simply be with Granddaddy. Those Sunday afternoons in his living room made an indelible impression on me. Without any verbal communication, the deep realization I received in Granddaddy's presence was that "When I am with Granddaddy, everything is OK. I can relax. Nothing can harm me." There was just a comforting vibe that he carried that had a deep effect on everyone around him.

Prayer is not simply speaking to God and listening for God's voice. Certainly verbal communication is vital to prayer, as it is in any relationship. But prayer is also communing with God. This is the experience of quieting ourselves, bringing stillness to our activity, and committing ourselves to simply be with God even in wordless silence.

In my experience, this is the most powerful form of prayer. And yet, it is also perhaps the most neglected in the American evangelical world.

As Western people, we tend to be driven by achievement and production. Therefore, we are often tormented by the fear that we don't have enough time in the day to do all that needs to be done. So we do everything in a hurry. We drive faster, work faster, talk faster, and read faster. We hate anything that causes us to wait. The thought of simply sitting quietly and doing nothing appears almost inconceivable.

This is precisely the mentality we must confront and intentionally revolt against in prayer, and one of the most effective ways this is done is through silent prayer. In silent prayer, we intentionally withdraw from the noise and activity of everyday life to be fully present to God.

> *"We must ruthlessly eliminate hurry from our lives. This does not mean we will never have things to do. Jesus often had much to do, but he never did it in a way that severed the life-giving connection between him and his Father. He never did it in a way that interfered with his ability to give love when love was called for. He observed a regular practice of withdrawing from activity for the sake of solitude and prayer." – John Ortberg*

Followers of Jesus understand that our value does not originate with our level of production or busyness. Our value comes from the reality that we are children of God, who loves us passionately, as he demonstrated concretely through the cross of Christ. Therefore, the most important use of my time each and every day is to simply sit with Jesus, resting in his love.

JESUS AND SOLITUDE

Jesus is baptized by his cousin, John, in the Jordan River in front of a sizable crowd of onlookers. As he emerges from the water, an ethereal voice speaks over him from above: "You are my son, whom I love; with you I am well pleased" (Luke 3:22, NIV).

Two things strike me about this statement. First, notice who the statement is directed to: Jesus himself. Not the crowds. I am sure the crowds benefitted from hearing the voice and experiencing this powerful moment. But the statement is made to Jesus, primarily for *his* benefit. *"You are my son. I love you. I am so pleased with you."*

Secondly, this dynamic encounter occurs at the very beginning of Jesus' public ministry. At this moment, he hasn't even preached his first sermon. He hasn't performed any signs, wonders, or miracles of any kind. No blind eyes have been opened. No demonized people have been set free. No hungry multitudes have been fed. Jesus is just some relatively anonymous carpenter's son from the tiny village of Nazareth.

And yet, the Father pronounces upon him this beautiful declaration of his loving affirmation.

Imagine you were stepping out into ministry today. You haven't accomplished anything yet. You haven't preached any sermons or taught any classes. You haven't visited any prisoners or hospital patients. You haven't led any small group sessions or outreach efforts. You haven't achieved anything worth measuring or celebrating in any way.

Yet, a cloud zips over you and you hear the voice of your heavenly Father say, "*You are my child. I love you so much. I am so proud of you.*" Pause for a moment. Maybe even put this book down. Hear him speak that over you right now.

The only thing you will *ever actually need* is the Father's loving affirmation. Everything else pales in comparison. John tells us that "God is love" (1 John 4:8, 16). Love is not simply one of God's many attributes. Love is his very essence. Everything God says and does flows out of his love; even his judgment. It can be no other way. Therefore, every time we connect with God we are connecting with the very essence and source of love, God himself.

If we can learn how to daily draw from the bottomless well of the Father's love, we will be fully empowered to become exactly who he has called us to be without the fear of others' opinions.

But if we do not learn how to do that, nothing else will be enough. No amount of ministry "success" or impressive accomplishments will consistently soothe the ache inside of us. His loving affirmation must become our exclusive source of identity, worth, and value. Otherwise, by default we will attempt to draw a sense of worth and identity from others, feeding off of the very people we are called to love sacrificially.

And this can happen in a couple different ways. First, we can attempt to self-medicate by attacking others, hoping to gain a sense of worth by diminishing someone else's value.

Or we can try to garner worth from the affirmation of others. "That was an awesome sermon, Pastor!" "You did a fantastic job serving at that outreach!" "I love the way you worship Jesus!"

Kind words of affirmation are certainly pleasant to give and receive. But there is a fine line between enjoying affirmation and developing an unhealthy dependence upon it. When we *depend* upon the support of others to give ourselves a sense of identity and value, we will eventually compromise our ministry and blunt our prophetic edge as a witness for Christ. Even without knowing it, we can warp our message according to how we think people will receive it.

This is something Jesus never did. He was completely free to always say and do exactly what the Father desired, regardless of how people might respond. Sometimes they loved him and flocked to him in droves. Other times they despised him and abandoned him. And of course, ultimately they would crucify him. Nevertheless, Jesus was fully empowered to be his Father's mouthpiece regardless of what the opinion polls said about him.

This could only happen because Jesus was totally secure in his identity and worth. "You are my son, whom I love; with you I am well pleased."

It wasn't only that one, single experience at the Jordan River. As documented throughout the gospels, it was Jesus' consistent practice throughout his life to break away from the noise, the activity, and even the distraction of "success" and find solitude with his Father.

And rising very early in the morning, while it was still dark, he departed and went out to a desolate place, and there he prayed (Mark 1:35).

It was during these frequent times of solitude and stillness that the Father was able to re-fuel Jesus with his loving presence, re-affirming his identity. This was the key to Jesus' fruitful ministry - his divine connection with his Father. Everywhere Jesus went he carried a deep reservoir of the Father's love that was constantly overflowing upon the people around him, even the ones who proclaimed themselves to be his enemies.

But the container for this reservoir of the Father's love was the practice of solitude. To put it another way, it was Jesus' commitment to solitude in his Father's loving presence that kept him secure in his identity, leaving him with nothing to prove, empowering him to live in love for each and every person he encountered—including the very ones who nailed him to the cross.

This is why the practices of silence and stillness are indispensable to our growth in the kingdom life. With the help of the Holy Spirit, these are practices that can enable us to do what we cannot do otherwise by our own self-effort. Jesus said it like this:

"I am the vine; you are the branches. If you remain in me and I in you, you will bear much fruit; apart from me you can do nothing" (John 15:5, NIV).

We cannot consistently bear the fruit of Christ-like love, mercy, and forgiveness as long as we depend on our own willpower and strategy. This fruit can only be produced as we learn how to simply remain in the Father's love. The practice of silent prayer is where we can find and foster that connection.

So every day in the middle of my morning prayer regimen, I have learned to embrace a period of silent prayer in God's loving presence. During this time I intentionally limit my speech and relax my thoughts. My only objective is to simply remain present to God.

In a world in which a thousand different things constantly compete for my attention, I am choosing to be still and quiet, doing nothing but rest in him. This is medicine for my soul.

"Who could believe that gently and without exertion we can receive our nourishment as a babe receives his milk? Yet, the more peaceful the child remains, the more nourishment he receives.

He may even fall asleep while nursing. This is how your spirit should be in prayer. Peaceful, relaxed, and without effort." –Madame Guyon

It is in my time of quiet rest in God's loving presence that I am in connection with the true source of my identity and worth. My worth does not come from my level of activity or my degree of "ministry success," however that may be defined. My worth comes solely from the fact that I am a child of God, made in his image, and redeemed by the blood of Jesus Christ. Therefore, I know that I have unsurpassable worth because Jesus paid an unsurpassable price on my behalf.

During this time of communing with God, I am not trying to "attain" God's presence because he is already present. I am simply withdrawing from the noise and activity of life in order to give time and space to enjoy his loving presence, which is all I will ever actually need. In his book, *Flee, Be Silent, Pray*, Ed Cyzewski writes:

> *"Learning to pray isn't about turning on the tap of God's love. Rather, learning to pray is about training ourselves to be present for the love of God that is already at work in our lives."*

In my daily practice of silent prayer, sometimes I have powerful encounters with God that have a deep, emotional impact. Occasionally, I sense God giving me encouragement or direction in a profound way. But on some days, there may not be anything notable that happens.

Someone in my church once came to me feeling troubled, saying, "When I practice silent prayer, most of the time I don't feel like I am getting anything out of it. Am I doing something wrong?"

The truth is, communing with God is not strictly about "getting results." Over time, the results will come. But our purpose in practicing solitude is not about what we can get out of it. Our intention is to simply be with God. As a young boy it would never have occurred to me to declare after an afternoon of watching TV with Granddaddy, "I didn't get anything out of that."

Perhaps the results are not the point. Maybe the results are secondary. The primary benefit of silent prayer is that we get to be with our loving Father. In him we lack nothing.

DISCUSSION QUESTIONS
CHAPTER THREE

1. Do you consistently make room for quiet rest in God's presence? If so, what are your experiences like?

2. Why is it such a challenge for us as Western people to be comfortable with silence and stillness? Try to consider both internal and external factors.

3. What counterfeit sources of worth and identity are you tempted to draw from? How might silent prayer be useful in this regard?

4. What are some practical arrangements you will need to make to begin creating space for practicing silence and stillness this week?

CHAPTER FOUR
PIGS IN A BLANKET

"I was in the city of Joppa praying, and in a trance I saw a vision…" (Acts 11:5a)

Roughly ten years after the outpouring of the Holy Spirit on the Day of Pentecost, this is how Simon Peter thinks about matters of faith: "God is the God of Jews only. Jesus is the Messiah for Jews only. The kingdom of God is the reign of God among Jews only."

We shouldn't be critical of Peter for thinking this way. It is literally impossible at this point in his life for him to think otherwise. This is how he has been formed and trained in scripture his entire life. If you were to ask Peter about the inclusion of Gentiles, his answer would be quite simple.

He'd say something like: "They can become Jews. Let them be circumcised. Let them begin to observe the Torah. And then they can have access to the Jewish

God, the Jewish Messiah, and the Jewish kingdom." At this point, this is how Peter thinks. He cannot think otherwise.

Then one day, Peter is in Joppa, the ancient seaside village south of what is now the modern city of Tel Aviv. He is staying in the home of Simon the Tanner. It's noon, Peter is hungry, and a meal is being prepared. As the food is cooking, he goes up onto the rooftop of the house for a time of prayer. The Jewish custom (which became the Christian custom) was to have fixed times of prayer throughout the day. It is now time for the noonday prayers to be prayed.

So Peter is on the roof. He is praying the prayers. He is also aware of his hunger. He can probably smell the meal that is being prepared.

But as he is praying, something unusual happens. He goes into what in English is most commonly translated as a "trance." It comes from the Greek word "*ekstasis*," from which we get the word "ecstasy." It means "to stand outside oneself." Or perhaps we can put it this way: "to get outside of what has always been one's frame of view."

So Peter is in this ecstatic, "trance-like" state. He then has a vision. And in this vision, a great sheet is lowered down from the heavens filled with what I as a Gentile would consider the possibility for a wonderful meal. Maybe there is a pig. A rabbit, perhaps. Possibly some shellfish. Lobsters. Crabs. Shrimp.

And the voice from heaven says, "Rise, Peter. Kill and eat." But Peter knows what this is. At least he thinks he knows. He assumes that this is a test of his commitment to keeping the Jewish dietary laws. He has been an observant Jew all his life.

And so Peter says, "Not so, Lord. Nothing unclean has ever entered my mouth." And he expects the voice to say, "Well done, Peter. You have passed the test."

But to his surprise, the voice in the vision says, "What God has called clean, you shall no more call unclean."

"Huh?....That wasn't what I was expecting."

And it's repeated three times. "Rise, Peter. Kill and eat."

"Not so, Lord. Nothing unclean has ever entered my mouth."

"What God has called clean, you shall no more call unclean." Three times.

As he is pondering this, there is a knock at the door. Standing at the doorstep is a delegation of Gentiles that has been sent on a couple days' journey from Caesarea by a Roman military officer. This centurion, a man named Cornelius, has had his own mystical experience involving an angel and has been instructed to send to Joppa at the house of Simon the Tanner and request that one Simon Peter come and explain something about Jesus.

If they had arrived an hour earlier, Peter would have probably declined. But he had just had this strange experience, hearing the voice of God say, "What you've been calling unclean, stop calling unclean." So he consents to go. He travels north to Caesarea with this delegation, bringing some of his own people with him.

And what follows is one of the most significant moments in all of church history. It is the moment that Simon Peter, the one entrusted with the keys to the kingdom, for the first time in his life crosses the threshold into a Gentile world. He has never done this before. He has never been inside of a Gentile house in his entire life.

He enters the home and begins talking about Jesus. And right in the middle of his talk, there is a repeat of

Pentecost. The same outpouring of the Holy Spirit that happened roughly ten years earlier in the Upper Room in Jerusalem is now happening in the villa of Cornelius, the Roman Centurion.

And Peter essentially says to himself, "What am I to do? If God is going to pour out his Spirit upon these Gentiles like he did in the Upper Room, who am I to say they can't belong?"

So he baptizes them, formally inducting them into the body of Messiah *as Gentiles*! They are not circumcised. There is no conversation about them keeping Torah. He just takes these pork chop-eating Gentiles and inducts them into the Jewish body of Messiah.

Of course, news gets back to Jerusalem pretty quickly, even before Peter has time to return. When Peter finally arrives, there is this faction waiting for him with folded arms and tapping toes. They are identified as the "circumcision party." Quite the oxymoron.

"What are you doing, Peter? You went to the home of uncircumcised Gentiles? And you ate with them!? And received them into the Jewish body of Messiah!? This is a slippery slope! You can't do that!"

And Peter replies, "I know...I know...I would agree... but I had this *experience*. I was in the city of Joppa praying, and in a trance I saw a vision. A new way of looking at Gentiles. And then I went, and there was a repeat of Pentecost. Who am I to argue?"

So Peter defends his decision to engage with Gentiles as equally deserving recipients of the grace of God in Christ on the basis of a mystical experience in prayer. He doesn't know how to justify it theologically. That task will later fall to the Apostle Paul as he pens his letter to the Christians in Rome—Paul's greatest theological project.

But this unprecedented and highly significant moment comes on the heels of Peter's contemplative breakthrough on a rooftop in Joppa. A moment in prayer that radically shifts his entire perspective.

RELEASING PRAYER TO THE HOLY SPIRIT

When we enter into communion with God through silence and stillness, we are yielding ourselves to the Holy Spirit in a way that has the potential to radically change our way of looking at the world.

Let's assume I am having a major disagreement with someone in my neighborhood. This person is saying nasty things about me to my neighbors around me. It's one thing for me to stew over it in prayer and angrily say, "God, show them how wrong they are!" But when I sit with Jesus in silence, now I am surrendering control of the moment to him. In his loving presence, he now has a chance to disarm my ego and my defensive mechanisms. And now it's possible for him to give me a 360(perspective of the issue. In this environment, now I am able to receive a word of wisdom over the matter and respond appropriately in a Christ-like posture.

As long as you remain firmly in control of your own prayer, you will never see the world differently than you already do. Instead, at some point in prayer each day, it is a healthy practice for us to surrender the time and space necessary to encounter God in wordless prayer, relinquishing our own efforts and submitting to whatever agenda the Holy Spirit may have.

When I am still and silent before God, I become stripped of my own agenda and my own toxic way of thinking. As the love of God permeates my mind, will, and emotions, all of the old attitudes of bitterness, selfishness, envy, and judgmentalism begin to dissipate and give way to peace, contentment, and wisdom from the Holy Spirit.

In this simple act of sitting quietly with him, I am fully at his mercy. By choosing silence, I am recognizing that I cannot engineer my own transformation. Transformation is the business of the Father. And by being fully present to him, I am giving him space and opportunity to do what only he can do. In his loving presence, he is reforming my inmost attitudes towards people, the circumstances of my life, and the world around me.

This notion of getting away from people to commune with God may sound selfish to the uninitiated. But properly understood, it is anything but selfish.

> *"The fruit of solitude is increased sensitivity and compassion for others." –Richard Foster*

As we make a daily habit of sitting in solitude with Jesus, we will inevitably become more attentive to the needs of the people in our lives. We will be formed into people who are calm, content, wise, and unafraid. As such, we are then enabled to properly respond to the world around us in a Christ-like posture.

But if we are not anchored by the practices of silence and stillness, we will be more easily sucked into the selfish currents of our internal appetites and external circumstances, often at the expense of others.

Before we look at some practical suggestions on how to engage in silent prayer, it must be stressed that we must first begin with the right expectation. The truth is you will probably not receive a major epiphany from God every single time you sit quietly with the Lord. In fact, those experiences may be relatively rare. There will be lots of times when it seems like nothing is happening. This is perfectly normal.

For American Evangelicals in general, and particularly for those of us who are of the Pentecostal/Charismatic variety, we can tend to be anxious and impatient, wanting to see evidence of growth every single time we pray. We want measurable results. We get easily distracted and impatient when we feel like we are being unproductive.

Impatience is an enemy to healthy prayer. When I first planted my muscadine grapevine, I watered it every day and fertilized it every few days. Every morning I would crouch down and stare at that vine hoping to see *some* evidence of growth. After the first three weeks, I was discouraged because nothing seemed to be happening. I worried that maybe there was something wrong with the vine. However, over the course of the next several months, the vine flourished and exceeded my expectations.

The work of spiritual growth is slow and unhurried. It is an organic process. We cannot control it or manage it. We can only submit to it and cooperate with it. Certainly we have our role. There is work involved. But ultimately the Holy Spirit is the one who brings the growth and increase. Sometimes we will see visible results; other times we will not.

But even when it seems like nothing is happening on the surface, we have to trust the work of the Holy Spirit. His work in our lives is deep and all-encompassing. Sometimes he impacts us on the level of our thoughts and emotions, therefore we can perceive his work. Yet other times his work is much deeper, reaching into the very root system of our hearts, on a level that may be imperceptible to us.

Our job is to simply release control, allow him full access, and choose to let go of our expectation to see and feel results every time. If we will submit to the process, results will certainly come. But those results are the product of a slow process that requires commitment and cooperation. And usually the results only become noticeable in ordinary life situations.

The power of prayer rests not in our words but in our connection to the Father. He is the one who produces love, peace, hope, and change. Our task is not to manufacture those realities, but to simply make time and space to remain connected to him.

PRACTICAL TIPS ON SILENT PRAYER

Learning how to engage in silent prayer can be a bit like learning how to swim. There are certainly helpful suggestions to offer, but ultimately you must *get in the water* and learn by *doing it*. With that said, here are some beneficial points of advice I can give you.

I would suggest getting in whatever posture helps you to focus. I have found that the posture of my body often affects my inward state. For example, normally when I sit I tend to slouch, but when I practice silence prayer before God, I like to sit with my spine straightened, my feet flat on the ground, and with my palms resting on my knees and open before the Lord. This helps me to remain attentive and alert. It also communicates respect and reverence. If the President of the United States were to walk into the room, I would never slouch in my seat with my legs crossed and my arms folded.

But there is no "rule" about prayer posture. Throughout Scripture we see examples of people praying in a variety of postures, everything from laying prostrate on the ground to standing straight gazing into the sky. There is no particular way it *must* be done. But I would suggest getting in a comfortable posture that will help relieve your mind from distraction.

When I begin my time of silent prayer, I like to begin by taking a few deep breaths to help me relax. Often I will close my eyes during this time. Occasionally, I might gaze upon a small cross I have in my office. If I am at home on my balcony, I like to look at the trees in my front yard. Regardless, my goal during this time is to give my full attention to my loving Father and behold his beauty and glory in the face of Christ.

I seek to engage in this practice for about twenty minutes every day in the middle of my morning prayer time. When you first begin doing this consistently, you will probably need to start small, perhaps beginning with five minutes a day. It is a bit like starting a jogging routine. In the beginning, you must start with jogging shorter distances with the goal of building up enough strength and endurance to run longer distances.

There is nothing magical about twenty minutes. I just find that twenty minutes of silent prayer is a great baseline. Twenty minutes is enough time to settle in and quiet the monkeys in my mind. The rest of my day will be so full of noise and activity that I need those twenty minutes of quiet rest in God's presence to keep me centered. And even throughout the rest of the day, at certain times I like to take another moment or two of solitude with God.

Imagine spending a large block of time every day watching your favorite television sitcom. Eventually the tone and character of that program will begin to flow into your life. Or imagine spending a significant amount of time every day browsing through shopping websites. In time you will develop an intense craving to acquire more possessions. We tend to crave what we consume, and therefore we consume what we crave.

If we want a craving for God's presence and the life that he brings, we must be willing to spend considerable time with him. If we do so, this practice will begin to have a profound impact on the way we think and live. We will be calmer, more content, and less anxious.

When you first begin practicing silent prayer with God, your soul may be quite resistant. In our noise-addicted society, we are a people for whom solitude does not come easy. However, over time, the more you practice solitude, the more you crave it, and it may even become your favorite part of the day.

While I do aim for twenty minutes a day, I certainly don't want the length of time I spend in silent prayer to become a point of fixation. Early on, when I first began practicing silent prayer before the Lord, I would put on a timer. This was helpful in the beginning. But now, I am a little more relaxed on the time length. There are certain days when I sense I am ready to move forward after ten or fifteen minutes. There are other days when I may want to go longer than twenty minutes and not hurry into the next segment of prayer. The point is to simply allow ourselves enough time to enjoy his presence. You never want your movement in prayer to feel constrained or forced. There should be a feeling of gentle peace as we move forward with each component of prayer.

Now during this time of silent prayer, this may be a time when the Holy Spirit speaks to you. Remember that hearing from God is a passive rather than an active process. If he has something to communicate, he will do so. But there is no need to grasp for anything. Simply rest in God's love and give him your full attention.

It doesn't happen every single time, but I have often received clear direction from God during these quiet moments. It may be a message of life-giving encouragement.

Early in my pastoral experience, our church was facing a season of significant financial pressure. I remember a moment when I was sitting on my balcony in prayer, feeling quite overwhelmed with the situation, and to be honest, I was also feeling ill-suited for my role. But as I sat with Jesus in silence, I brought my thoughts and feelings before him. And the following words entered my mind with striking clarity:

I love you.
You are my chosen one for this hour.
Come find your rest in me.
Don't get entangled by the minutia.
The most important use of your time is being with me.

I will never forget that experience. I am always reluctant to ascribe God's voice to something and say, "God told me…" But I make no apologies for stating that this was a clear and unmistakable message from God for me in that moment. That experience in prayerful solitude was my lifeline that carried me through that difficult season.

If God speaks to you in these moments of silence, it won't always be a highly emotional experience. Oftentimes he may give simple instruction regarding how to relate to your spouse or a friend at work. He may lovingly expose a negative thought pattern or a selfish attitude towards a difficult person in your life. Through these consecrated times of solitude with Jesus, he can form and shape us to be people who live in love for each and every person we encounter.

Often I will use part of this time to reflect on a certain passage of scripture. Maybe there is a certain verse or phrase that I feel impressed to ponder in my heart. This isn't a time for deep study or analysis, but to simply encounter God. For those who are part of the Pentecostal/Charismatic movement, this can also be an ideal time to spend a few moments using your prayer language.

I have found these times of silence can be quite unique. There are all kinds of wonderful things that can happen. But the key is to commit yourself to the practice on a daily basis. Occasionally you will have unforgettable "mountain-top" encounters with God. However, more often than not these times will seem ordinary and unremarkable. Don't get discouraged. Enjoy his loving presence. The only thing you can do wrong is give up and walk out.

And of course, you will encounter distracting thoughts. This is perfectly normal. Whenever you find yourself lost in thought, take a moment and evaluate the nature of the distraction. Perhaps it may be an issue you need to bring before God. Perhaps you're anxious over a meeting you will have later in the day. Rather than attempt to fight against that thought, perhaps the Holy Spirit wants you to surrender the issue before him.

On the other hand, you will also have inane thoughts that are just plain distractions ("I wonder what I'll have for lunch today."). When I catch myself in one of these thoughts, I find it helpful to just say the name "Jesus." It re-focuses my attention. This may happen multiple times in one sitting. But don't feel guilty about it. Over time the frequency of these distracting thoughts will decrease. But when one of these thoughts pops into your mind, just acknowledge the distraction for what it is and return to him.

I will close with this wonderful quote from Richard Foster:

"Be patient with yourself…you are learning a discipline for which you have received no training. Nor does our culture encourage you to develop these skills. You will be going against the tide, but take heart; your task is of immense worth."

DISCUSSION QUESTIONS

CHAPTER FOUR

1. Describe the steps you took this week to begin incorporating silence into your prayer life.

2. What were the distractions that came? How did you respond to them?

3. How did you experience God in your times of silence this week?

4. What cares or concerns do you need to entrust more deeply to God in order to be fully present to him during these times of silence and solitude?

5. What was your biggest takeaway from this chapter on silent prayer?

CHAPTER FIVE
MORNING PRAYER TRELLIS

We will now walk through the elements of the "prayer trellis" that I use every morning. I understand everyone's prayer trellis can be unique. Some readers may prefer something a little simpler. Or you may prefer to use other components not included. There is certainly more than one way to do this. But if you don't already have a prayer trellis, I highly recommend trying this one.

It includes every element we have discussed in previous chapters: improvised prayer, silent prayer, various passages of Scripture, as well as a collection of beautiful prayers that have been handed down to us by our brothers and sisters in Christ from previous generations.

I first received a version of this prayer trellis from Brian Zahnd, the pastor of Word of Life Church in St. Joseph, Missouri. I have made several modifications.

But each section is carefully arranged to facilitate a natural movement of prayer.

I cannot emphasize enough the importance of praying with slow, thoughtful reflection. There is no benefit to mindless repetition. Slow down enough to allow the words to absorb into your heart and mind. Before you begin, take a deep breath. Welcome the involvement of the Holy Spirit. Don't expect obvious, tangible results every single time. True lasting, spiritual growth is a slow and patient work.

It will probably take a minimum of thirty minutes to pray through the entire thing. However, that depends upon your pace as well as the length of time you take in the "improvisational prayer" and "silent prayer" sections. Over time, you may find yourself willing and capable enough to spend an hour or two in prayer, if you so choose.

For the first few days (or weeks, perhaps), using this prayer trellis may feel strange and awkward. Especially for those who may be using structure for the first time. It can be like trying on a new pair of running shoes. It will feel stiff and uncomfortable at first. But over time and with enough use, you will settle into it, and it will become your own. For that reason, I would encourage you not to evaluate it until you have used it for at least three weeks. You will need time to "break it in."

One thing that will help you tremendously is if you will commit to memorizing as much as you can. Perhaps you can make it a goal to memorize two or three lines a day. Memorization will help you internalize what you are praying. It will begin to take root in your heart. For this reason, I also urge you to pray out loud. Rather than simply using your thoughts, get your voice involved. Speak it out. Hear yourself saying the words.

And please remember to follow the leading of the Holy Spirit. There may be moments when you should pause and reflect. Or times when you should deviate from "the script." There may be an instant when you feel impressed to use your heavenly prayer language. Whatever the case, if at any point you feel restricted or constrained, you may be either lacking focus or moving too fast. Slow down, engage your heart and mind, and cooperate with the Holy Spirit. Rightfully understood, the prayer trellis is meant to usher us into those encounters.

I encourage you to find a "prayer spot." Choose a consistent place around your home or office which you can designate as a sacred spot. If you pray indoors, you may find it helpful to sit by a window, light a candle, or surround yourself with objects of beauty (a painting or a small cross, for example). I have a couple playlists of soft, worshipful music that I like to play in the background. These are the types of things that can potentially enrich our times of prayer with God.

Now let's walk through each component of the morning prayer trellis that I use. I will give commentary to help explain each section. You will find a simplified version of this prayer trellis without commentary in the Appendix.

OPENING ADDRESS

FATHER GOD, CREATOR OF HEAVEN AND EARTH,
GOD OF ABRAHAM, ISAAC, AND JACOB,
GOD OF ISRAEL,
GOD AND FATHER OF OUR LORD AND SAVIOR JESUS CHRIST,
TRUE AND LIVING GOD WHO IS FATHER, SON, AND HOLY SPIRIT,
HAVE MERCY AND HEAR OUR PRAYER.

As we begin, we clearly identify whom we are communicating with, with a deep sense of awe and reverence. Each line of this address (written by Brian

Zahnd) takes us through the progression of biblical revelation. He is our Creator (Genesis 1-2). He established a covenant to redeem the world through the descendants of Abraham (Genesis 12). He chose a people for himself through whom he would reveal himself to the nations (the entirety of the Hebrew Scriptures). He fulfilled the mission of Israel through the person, ministry, and work of his son Jesus Christ (the new covenant). And he has revealed himself as a triune God who is at work in the world today (the church age).

Rather than beginning the prayer casually and flippantly ("Hey God…"), it is appropriate for us to begin with honor and respect, reminding ourselves that we are part of a movement of revelation that has been taking place since the beginning of time itself.

DOXOLOGY

PRAISE GOD, FROM WHOM ALL BLESSING FLOW;
PRAISE HIM, ALL CREATURES HERE BELOW;
PRAISE HIM ABOVE, YE HEAVENLY HOST;
PRAISE FATHER, SON, AND HOLY GHOST!

PSALM 103:1-5; 1

Bless the Lord, O my soul,
and all that is within me,
bless his holy name!
Bless the Lord, O my soul,
and forget not all his benefits,
who forgives all your iniquity,
who heals all your diseases,
who redeems your life from the pit,
who crowns you with steadfast love and mercy,
who satisfies you with good
so that your youth is renewed like the eagle's.
Bless the Lord, O my soul,
and all that is within me,
bless his holy name!

It is vital right at the beginning of our prayer to behold the beauty of God. To bask in his beauty. So take a few moments and praise him. I like to begin with the Doxology as well as a section of Psalm 103 every morning. But I will also "ad lib" some, and express praise to God with my own vocabulary. Occasionally I will include the words of a verse from a hymn, poem, or worship song. Whatever the case, this is a time to cast your affections upon God and allow your heart to swell with gratitude, expressing praise to him.

JESUS PRAYER

*LORD JESUS CHRIST, SON OF GOD,
HAVE MERCY ON ME [A SINNER].*

The "Jesus Prayer" is a one-sentence prayer that dates back to the desert mothers and fathers from 1,700 years ago. But ultimately its roots are in the gospels themselves. In one of Jesus' parables, a Pharisee and a tax collector enter into the temple. The Pharisee's prayer is self-righteous and arrogant: "*God, I thank you that I am not like other men, extortioners, unjust, adulterers, or even like this tax collector. I fast twice a week; I give tithes of all that I get*" (Luke 18:11-12).

By contrast, the tax collector is too broken to even lift his head to pray. He pounds his chest and mutters this simple line: "*God, be merciful to me, a sinner*" (v. 13). Jesus finishes the parable with this sobering line: "*I tell you, this man went down to his house justified, rather than the other. For everyone who exalts himself will be humbled, but the one who humbles himself will be exalted*" (v. 14).

There are many similar pleas found in Jesus' ministry:

"*Have mercy on us, Son of David!*" *(Matthew 9:27)*

> *"Have mercy on me, O Lord, Son of David!" (Matthew 15:22)*
> *"Lord, have mercy on my son..." (Matthew 17:15)*
> *"Lord, have mercy on us, Son of David!" (Matthew 20:30-31)*
> *"Jesus, Son of David, have mercy on me!" (Mark 17:13)*
> *"Jesus, Master, have mercy on us!" (Luke 17:13)*

Of course, there is nothing magical about the words themselves. But it is the posture of a humble heart that attracts God's attention. We must live with an understanding that apart from the mercy of God, we have nothing to stand upon. For that reason, I like to sprinkle in the Jesus Prayer several times throughout the prayer trellis. It is there to condition us to keep our hearts in a place of humility, gratitude, and reverence.

In this first occurrence of the Jesus Prayer, you will notice the words "a sinner" in brackets at the end. This is because it leads into the following section, which is a confession of sin.

CONFESSION OF SIN

MOST MERCIFUL GOD,
WE CONFESS THAT WE HAVE SINNED AGAINST YOU
IN THOUGHT, WORD, AND DEED,
BY WHAT WE HAVE DONE,
AND BY WHAT WE HAVE LEFT UNDONE.
WE HAVE NOT LOVED YOU WITH OUR WHOLE HEART;
WE HAVE NOT LOVED OUR NEIGHBORS AS OURSELVES.
WE ARE TRULY SORRY AND WE HUMBLY REPENT.
FOR THE SAKE OF YOUR SON JESUS CHRIST,
HAVE MERCY ON US AND FORGIVE US;
THAT WE MAY DELIGHT IN YOUR WILL,
AND WALK IN YOUR WAYS
TO THE GLORY OF YOUR NAME.

You may have observed that this prayer is pluralized. Sometimes I will pray this prayer in the singular ("Most merciful God, *I* confess that *I* have sinned against you..."). But most of the time I like to keep it in the plural, just as it is in the Lord's Prayer ("Forgive *us*...as *we* forgive...").

There is a very important reason for this. First, it is a revolt against our tendency to individualize our Christian experience. In the American West, ours is a hyper-individualistic society. We place a premium value on independence. Many of us can live across the street from neighbors for years without ever actually meeting them or spending any time with them.

As Christians, if we are not careful, we can conform our faith to this cultural pattern. And it becomes all about *me* and *my* personal, "private" relationship with Jesus. Christianity is not a lone ranger sport. We are members of the *body* of Christ. We are in this thing together.

When we fall into this individualistic mindset, we can tend to think of sin in that fashion. We consider sin to be only that for which we are personally, individually culpable. Of course, we do need to confess our personal, individual sin to the Lord. But if we stop there we ignore an entire category of sin that we might call "systemic sin."

For example, what if the shirt you may be wearing right now was made in a sweatshop in Guatemala by people making pennies a day? Of course, I'm not trying to heap condemnation on anyone. I am only attempting to make you aware of the fact that there are all kinds of ways we can benefit from *systems* of sin, whether we know it or not. And sometimes these systems of sin can be extremely difficult, if not impossible, for us to fully disentangle ourselves from. So what do we do about it? There may be all kinds of things we should do about it. But from the very start, we must confess it in prayer. "Most merciful God, *we* confess that *we* have sinned…"

At the end, feel free to also make space for individual confession of sin. This is an opportunity to make your confession more personal and specific.

PSALM FOR THE DAY

PSALM 23

The Lord is my shepherd; I shall not want.
He makes me lie down in green pastures.
He leads me beside still waters.
He restores my soul.
He leads me in paths of righteousness
for his name's sake.
Even though I walk through the valley of the
shadow of death,
I will fear no evil,
for you are with me;
your rod and your staff,
they comfort me.
You prepare a table before me

IN THE PRESENCE OF MY ENEMIES;
YOU ANOINT MY HEAD WITH OIL;
MY CUP OVERFLOWS.
SURELY GOODNESS AND MERCY SHALL FOLLOW ME
ALL THE DAYS OF MY LIFE,
AND I SHALL DWELL IN THE HOUSE OF THE LORD
FOREVER.

PSALM 91:1-2

HE WHO DWELLS IN THE SHELTER OF THE MOST HIGH
WILL ABIDE IN THE SHADOW OF THE ALMIGHTY.
I WILL SAY TO THE LORD, "MY REFUGE AND MY
FORTRESS,
MY GOD, IN WHOM I TRUST."

We don't merely read the psalms. We don't simply study the psalms. We *pray* the psalms. When we pray through the Book of Psalms, we are joining a tradition that has been ongoing for 3,000 years. The Book of Psalms is the definitive Jewish prayer book. The early Christians also used the psalms in this fashion. We know that Jesus himself prayed through the psalms and committed them to memory.

There are 150 psalms and 365 days a year. So if you pray through a psalm each day for an entire year, you will have prayed through the Book of Psalms roughly two and a half times (You can stay on track with the Psalm for the Day at *www.healthyprayer.com*).

Some of the psalms are joyful and uplifting. Others are gloomy and mournful. However, it is good practice to simply take them as they come. Don't pick and choose which psalm to use on a particular day based on your mood. The purpose of praying through the psalms is not to express how *you* feel, but to feel what *they* express.

For one thing, we must continually remind ourselves that we as individuals are not the center of the universe. We're part of the singular body of Christ as well as the larger human race. And though I may not be going through a miserable experience at this very moment, I have brothers and sisters in my church who may be dealing with the intense sorrow of losing a loved one. Or I may know of missionaries and believers in other nations who are enduring intense persecution. Or perhaps I am aware of someone who has recently received a devastating medical diagnosis. Therefore, in prayer we must solidify ourselves with others, rejoicing with those who rejoice and grieving with those who grieve.

Besides, even if I may not be experiencing personal sorrow right now, I can be certain that it will come eventually. Praying through the psalms on a daily basis is like digging a deep well that I can draw from when I *do* experience dark days. When we pray through the psalms, we are learning to process the full range of human emotions in a way that is healthy.

Now, I have to address one issue. You will notice that a few of the psalms are particularly violent. For example in Psalm 3:7, David writes, *"Arise, O LORD! Save me, O my God! For you strike all my enemies on the cheek; you break the teeth of the wicked."*

As followers of Jesus, we are taught to love our enemies and pray for our persecutors (Matthew 5:44). So if someone cuts me off in traffic on the interstate, the prayer that comes from my mouth should *not* be, "Lord, bash his teeth in!" But what do we do with these violent sections? It is, after all, part of holy Scripture. We can't just cut it out of our Bibles.

My practice is to spiritualize these particular verses. Rather than imagine someone else, I like to apply it to my spiritual enemies—the demonic powers and principalities that enslave people, torment families, and destroy destinies. "Lord, bash *their* teeth in!"

After the Psalm for the Day, I've included Psalm 23 and the first two lines of Psalm 91. As you continue to pray, remember to do so slowly with thoughtful reflection. Absorb every word.

PRAYER FOR FAMILY

A prayer for married couples:

LORD, GRANT ME THE STRENGTH TO ANSWER YOUR CALL TO BE A LIVING SIGN OF YOUR LOVE. MAKE MY LOVE FOR _____ TO BE LIKE YOUR LOVE FOR HIM/HER. PASSIONATE, PERMANENT, INTIMATE, UNCONDITIONAL, AND LIFE-GIVING. MAY I BE AS PRESENT TO _____ AS YOU ARE TO HIM/HER, SO THAT ALL THE WORLD CAN SEE YOUR PRESENCE MANIFESTED IN OUR TENDER LOVE FOR ONE ANOTHER. HELP US BOTH TO STAY CLOSE TO YOU IN THE BODY OF CHRIST, AND CONTINUE TO NOURISH OUR LOVE WITH YOUR LOVE. IN JESUS' NAME.

A prayer for singles:

LORD, GRANT ME THE STRENGTH TO ANSWER YOUR CALL TO BE A LIVING SIGN OF YOUR LOVE. MAKE MY LOVE FOR OTHERS TODAY REFLECT YOUR LOVE FOR ME:

LOYAL, FAITHFUL, UNCONDITIONAL, AND LIFE-GIVING. MAY I BE AS PRESENT TO OTHERS AS YOU ARE TO ME, SO THAT ALL THE WORLD CAN SEE YOUR PRESENCE MANIFESTED IN MY TENDER LOVE FOR OTHERS. HELP ME STAY CLOSE TO YOU IN THE BODY OF CHRIST. AND CONTINUE TO NOURISH MY LOVE WITH YOUR LOVE. IN JESUS' NAME.

A prayer for children:

ALMIGHTY GOD, HEAVENLY FATHER, YOU HAVE BLESSED US WITH JOY AND CARE OF CHILDREN. GIVE US CALM STRENGTH AND PATIENT WISDOM AS WE BRING THEM UP, THAT WE MAY TEACH THEM TO LOVE WHATEVER IS JUST AND TRUE AND GOOD, FOLLOWING THE EXAMPLE OF OUR SAVIOR, JESUS CHRIST.

If you prefer, this can be a time to offer your own improvised prayer for your family. However, I have also included some recommended prayers above, if you choose to use them. The first two prayers (for marrieds and singles) were written by Pete Scazzero, author of *The Emotionally Healthy Leader*. The third prayer (for children) comes from *The Book of Common Prayer*.

THE LORD'S PRAYER (KJV)

Our Father, who art in heaven,
hallowed be Thy name.
Thy kingdom come,
thy will be done
on earth as it is in heaven.
Give us this day our daily bread.
And forgive us our trespasses,
as we forgive those who trespass against us.
And lead us not into temptation,
but deliver us from evil.
For thine is the kingdom and the power
and the glory forever.
Amen.

THE LORD'S PRAYER (PERSONALIZED AND EXPANDED)

Here is where I include the Lord's Prayer twice. The first time I pray the Lord's Prayer as given in scripture. The second time, I loosen up a little and begin to pray extemporaneously, using the Lord's Prayer as a model. I take each line of the Lord's Prayer and put my own "spin" on it (ex. "…Holy is your name. May your name be respected and glorified. May your kingdom agenda be recognized and submitted to here and everywhere as in heaven…")

IMPROVISED PRAYER

Finally, this is your chance to play your "jazz piano solo." Offer your own words and requests to God. Intercede for others. This section can take as long as you wish, of course.

SILENT PRAYER

At this point, we are now ready to relinquish control of the prayer and sit quietly in solitude with Jesus (see Chapters 3 and 4). Everything we have done so far is designed to get us to this point. Again, this section can take as long as you'd like.

As wonderful as our prayer time with God can be, eventually we must return to our work, our homes, and our relationships. For this reason, the second half of the prayer trellis is designed to prepare us to re-enter society in a Christ-like posture.

PRAYER TO THE CRUCIFIED CHRIST

Lord Jesus, you stretched out your arms of love upon the hard wood of the cross that everyone might come within the reach of your saving embrace; so clothe us with your Spirit that we, reaching forth our hands in love, may bring those who don't know you to the knowledge and love of you; for the honor of your name.

BEATITUDES (MATTHEW 5:3-10)

*Blessed are the poor in spirit,
for theirs is the kingdom of heaven.
Blessed are those who mourn,
for they shall be comforted.
Blessed are the meek,
for they shall inherit the earth.
Blessed are those who hunger and thirst for righteousness,
for they shall be satisfied.
Blessed are the merciful,
for they shall receive mercy.
Blessed are the pure in heart,
for they shall see God.
Blessed are the peacemakers,
for they shall be called sons of God.*

*Blessed are those who are persecuted for righteousness' sake,
for theirs is the kingdom of heaven.*

PRAYER FOR PEACE (SHALOM)

O God, you have made of one blood all the peoples of the earth, and sent your blessed Son to preach peace to those who are far off and to those who are near; Grant that people everywhere may seek after you and find you; Bring the nations into your fold; Pour out your Spirit upon all flesh; and hasten the coming of your kingdom; through Jesus Christ our Lord.

PRAYER OF FRANCIS OF ASSISI

*Lord, make me an instrument of your peace,
Where there is hatred, let me sow love;
Where there is injury, pardon;
Where there is doubt, faith;
Where there is despair, hope;
Where there is darkness, light;
Where there is sadness, joy;
O Divine Master,
grant that I may not so much seek to be
consoled, as to console;*

TO BE UNDERSTOOD, AS TO UNDERSTAND;
TO BE LOVED, AS TO LOVE.
FOR IT IS IN GIVING THAT WE RECEIVE,
IT IS IN PARDONING THAT WE ARE PARDONED,
AND IT IS IN DYING THAT WE ARE BORN TO ETERNAL LIFE.

PRAYER FOR THE WEEK

Aside from the Beatitudes (which I find to be indispensable to my morning prayer time), this section also includes three beautifully composed prayers filled with rich, theological truth. Take your time with these prayers and allow them to shape your perspective for the day.

The "Prayer for the Week" element brings some variety to this section. These well-written, theologically-robust prayers have been enriching the hearts of Christians for hundreds of years. You can find them listed in the Appendix (the Prayer for the Week is also available at *www.healthyprayer.com*)

RYAN POST

PRAYER FOR GRACE

LORD GOD, ALMIGHTY AND EVERLASTING FATHER, YOU HAVE BROUGHT US IN SAFETY TO THIS NEW DAY. PRESERVE US WITH YOUR MIGHTY POWER, THAT WE MAY NOT FALL INTO SIN, NOR BE OVERCOME BY ADVERSITY; AND IN ALL WE DO, DIRECT US TO THE FULFILLING OF YOUR PURPOSE; THROUGH JESUS CHRIST OUR LORD.

PRAYER OF THANKSGIVING

*ALMIGHTY GOD, FATHER OF ALL MERCIES,
WE YOUR UNWORTHY SERVANTS GIVE YOU HUMBLE THANKS
FOR ALL YOUR GOODNESS AND LOVING-KINDNESS
TO US AND ALL WHOM YOU HAVE MADE.
WE BLESS YOU FOR OUR CREATION, PRESERVATION,
AND ALL THE BLESSINGS OF THIS LIFE;
BUT ABOVE ALL FOR YOUR IMMEASURABLE LOVE
IN THE REDEMPTION OF THE WORLD THROUGH OUR
LORD JESUS CHRIST;
FOR THE MEANS OF GRACE, AND FOR THE HOPE OF GLORY.
AND, WE PRAY, GIVE US SUCH AN AWARENESS OF YOUR MERCIES,
THAT WITH TRULY THANKFUL HEARTS WE MAY SHOW
FORTH YOUR PRAISE,
NOT ONLY WITH OUR LIPS, BUT IN OUR LIVES,
BY GIVING UP OUR SELVES TO YOUR SERVICE,
AND BY WALKING BEFORE YOU*

IN HOLINESS AND RIGHTEOUSNESS ALL OUR DAYS;
THROUGH JESUS CHRIST OUR LORD,
TO WHOM, WITH YOU AND THE HOLY SPIRIT,
BE HONOR AND GLORY THROUGHOUT ALL AGES.
AMEN.

DECLARATION OF VICTORY

CHRIST HAS DIED.
CHRIST IS RISEN.
CHRIST WILL COME AGAIN.

Near the end of the prayer trellis is a prayer for grace over our day along with a beautiful expression of thanksgiving. Every line is soaked with wonderful truth. Allow each word to descend into your heart.

We bring the prayer to a close with a joyful declaration of victory: "Christ has died. Christ is risen. Christ will come again." Amen!

DISCUSSION QUESTIONS
CHAPTER FIVE

1. Of the three main elements discussed in this book (structure, silence, and spontaneity), which of them has been most lacking in your prayer life?

2. Describe what your prayer time has been like over the last few days and weeks. Have you noticed any changes in the way you approach God in prayer?

3. After using this prayer trellis for the past several days and weeks, what has been your favorite component?

4. Are there any components you would like to add to your own prayer trellis?

AFTERWORD

The scope of this book has been mainly limited to describing the benefit and components of a healthy morning prayer regimen. I have made my best attempt to help readers grasp how beautiful prayer can be when we integrate structure, silence, and spontaneity.

However, I believe it is important for me to share a few words about engaging in prayer during other parts of the day. The apostle Paul encouraged us to "*pray without ceasing*" (1 Thessalonians 5:17). The Greek word for "without ceasing" (*adialeiptos*) doesn't mean "non-stop." It refers to a constant recurrence of prayer throughout one's day.

As I mentioned in Chapter 4, the early Christian custom was to have fixed times of prayer throughout the day. In fact, some streams of Christianity continue in this practice today. The intent of this practice is to keep coming back to God, stay centered in his love, and remain aware of his presence throughout the day regardless of daily tasks.

I have found that even with a healthy prayer regimen in the morning, I still need to engage in brief times of prayer throughout the day in order to remain in Christ and walk in love.

With this in mind, there are two other prayer exercises that I frequently use and highly recommend. Both of these methods have been around for hundreds of years. Each exercise usually takes just a few minutes.

LECTIO DIVINA

The first method is traditionally referred to as "*lectio divina*," a Latin term that simply means "divine reading." It's a way of encountering God in Scripture. There are several components to this exercise.

First, I take a short passage of Scripture and read it slowly and out loud. Usually the passage is no longer than 8-10 verses.

Then, I read it once more, and this time I allow God's Spirit to illuminate a particular word or phrase. At this point I am not trying to analyze the text. This is not a time for word studies. This is a time for listening to God speaking through Scripture.

Next, I sit quietly for about five minutes and meditate on the passage. I enter into the story. For example, suppose I am reflecting on the story of Jesus' baptism. I use my imagination to enter that scene. I feel the cool waters of the Jordan around my waist and the ray of sunshine across my face, imagining how Jesus may have felt receiving this beautiful affirmation from his Father.

Or perhaps I take a moment and put myself in the crowd watching this amazing historical moment. What would have gone through their minds? As I sit and reflect on the passage, I zero in on the truth I feel like God may be speaking to me.

Finally, I conclude with a brief verbal response to God followed with the Lord's Prayer. This prayer method helps me to encounter God through Scripture and keeps me centered in him in the midst of everyday activities.

THE EXAMEN

I like to use the second prayer exercise near the end of my day. The "examen" is a prayer exercise in which we learn from the events of the previous day. I like to call it "reflective prayer."

When I played baseball in high school, I can remember our coach periodically filming each player's swing during batting practice. The next day we would go to the locker room and watch each player's swing in slow motion, analyzing it for strengths and weaknesses.

This illustrates the purpose of reflective prayer. As we prayerfully look back on the previous day, we allow the Holy Spirit the opportunity to teach us. Here are a few steps that will help you in this exercise:

1. Take a deep breath and relax. Ask God to make his presence known around you and in you. Feel his presence and soak in it.

2. Ask God to fill you with his merciful love. Ask God to be the leader of this prayer time.

3. Ask God to reveal all the gifts and graces he has given you today, from the big ones to the small ones. Thank God for each of these gifts as they come to mind.

4. Going hour by hour, review your day. In your imagination, revisit each significant moment of your day. Linger in the important moments and pass quickly over the less relevant ones.

5. Continue thanking God for the gifts you find in your day. Pause at any of the difficult

moments of your day. Pay attention to any missed opportunities, when you could have acted in a certain way but didn't. When you find moments in which you missed the mark, ask God's forgiveness. Try to sense his healing mercy wash over you.

6. Ask God to show you, concretely, how he wants you to respond or what he wants you to do tomorrow. Ask God to show you what kind of person he is calling you to be tomorrow. Resolve to be that person and ask God for his help.

7. Ask yourself if there are any last words you wish to say to the Lord.

I have found these two prayer practices to bear good fruit in my life, and I highly recommend their use. They will help you remain connected to God throughout your day.

Spiritual growth does not happen automatically. We must be intentional about positioning ourselves to grow spiritually. Committing to prayer practices like these can help serve this purpose.

APPENDIX I

MORNING PRAYER TRELLIS (SIMPLIFIED)

OPENING ADDRESS

Father God, Creator of heaven and earth,
God of Abraham, Isaac, and Jacob,
God of Israel,
God and Father of our Lord and Savior Jesus Christ,
True and living God who is Father, Son, and Holy Spirit,
Have mercy and hear our prayer.

DOXOLOGY

Praise God, from whom all blessings flow;
Praise him, all creatures here below;
Praise him above, ye heavenly host;
Praise Father, Son, and Holy Ghost!

PSALM 103:1-5; 1

*Bless the Lord, O my soul,
and all that is within me,
bless his holy name!
Bless the Lord, O my soul,
and forget not all his benefits,
who forgives all your iniquity,
who heals all your diseases,
who redeems your life from the pit,
who crowns you with steadfast love and mercy,
who satisfies you with good
so that your youth is renewed like the eagle's.*

*Bless the Lord, O my soul,
and all that is within me,
bless his holy name!*

JESUS PRAYER

Lord Jesus Christ, Son of God, have mercy on me [a sinner].

CONFESSION OF SIN

*Most merciful God,
we confess that we have sinned against you
in thought, word, and deed,
by what we have done,
and by what we have left undone.*

WE HAVE NOT LOVED YOU WITH OUR WHOLE HEART;
WE HAVE NOT LOVED OUR NEIGHBORS AS OURSELVES.
WE ARE TRULY SORRY AND WE HUMBLY REPENT.
FOR THE SAKE OF YOUR SON JESUS CHRIST,
HAVE MERCY ON US AND FORGIVE US;
THAT WE MAY DELIGHT IN YOUR WILL,
AND WALK IN YOUR WAYS
TO THE GLORY OF YOUR NAME.

PSALM FOR THE DAY

JESUS PRAYER

PSALM 23

THE LORD IS MY SHEPHERD; I SHALL NOT WANT.
HE MAKES ME LIE DOWN IN GREEN PASTURES.
HE LEADS ME BESIDE STILL WATERS.
HE RESTORES MY SOUL.
HE LEADS ME IN PATHS OF RIGHTEOUSNESS
FOR HIS NAME'S SAKE.
EVEN THOUGH I WALK THROUGH THE VALLEY OF THE SHADOW OF DEATH,
I WILL FEAR NO EVIL,
FOR YOU ARE WITH ME;
YOUR ROD AND YOUR STAFF,
THEY COMFORT ME.
YOU PREPARE A TABLE BEFORE ME

IN THE PRESENCE OF MY ENEMIES;
YOU ANOINT MY HEAD WITH OIL;
MY CUP OVERFLOWS.
SURELY GOODNESS AND MERCY SHALL FOLLOW ME
ALL THE DAYS OF MY LIFE,
AND I SHALL DWELL IN THE HOUSE OF THE LORD
FOREVER.

PSALM 91:1-2
HE WHO DWELLS IN THE SHELTER OF THE MOST HIGH
WILL ABIDE IN THE SHADOW OF THE ALMIGHTY.
I WILL SAY TO THE LORD, "MY REFUGE AND MY FORTRESS,
MY GOD, IN WHOM I TRUST."

PRAYER FOR FAMILY

THE LORD'S PRAYER (KJV)
OUR FATHER, WHO ART IN HEAVEN,
HALLOWED BE THY NAME.
THY KINGDOM COME,
THY WILL BE DONE
ON EARTH AS IT IS IN HEAVEN.
GIVE US THIS DAY OUR DAILY BREAD.
AND FORGIVE US OUR TRESPASSES,
AS WE FORGIVE THOSE WHO TRESPASS AGAINST US.
AND LEAD US NOT INTO TEMPTATION,
BUT DELIVER US FROM EVIL.

*For thine is the kingdom and the power
and the glory forever.
Amen.*

Jesus Prayer

The Lord's Prayer (personalized and expanded)

Improvised Prayer

Silent Prayer

Prayer to the Crucified Christ
Lord Jesus, you stretched out your arms of love upon the hard wood of the cross that everyone might come within the reach of your saving embrace; so clothe us with your Spirit that we, reaching forth our hands in love, may bring those who don't know you to the knowledge and love of you; for the honor of your name.

Beatitudes (Matthew 5:3-10)
*Blessed are the poor in spirit,
for theirs is the kingdom of heaven.
Blessed are those who mourn,
for they shall be comforted.*

BLESSED ARE THE MEEK,
FOR THEY SHALL INHERIT THE EARTH.
BLESSED ARE THOSE WHO HUNGER AND THIRST FOR RIGHTEOUSNESS,
FOR THEY SHALL BE SATISFIED.
BLESSED ARE THE MERCIFUL,
FOR THEY SHALL RECEIVE MERCY.
BLESSED ARE THE PURE IN HEART,
FOR THEY SHALL SEE GOD.
BLESSED ARE THE PEACEMAKERS,
FOR THEY SHALL BE CALLED SONS OF GOD.
BLESSED ARE THOSE WHO ARE PERSECUTED FOR RIGHTEOUSNESS' SAKE,
FOR THEIRS IS THE KINGDOM OF HEAVEN.

PRAYER FOR PEACE (SHALOM)

O GOD, YOU HAVE MADE OF ONE BLOOD ALL THE PEOPLES OF THE EARTH, AND SENT YOUR BLESSED SON TO PREACH PEACE TO THOSE WHO ARE FAR OFF AND TO THOSE WHO ARE NEAR; GRANT THAT PEOPLE EVERYWHERE MAY SEEK AFTER YOU AND FIND YOU; BRING THE NATIONS INTO YOUR FOLD; POUR OUT YOUR SPIRIT UPON ALL FLESH; AND HASTEN THE COMING OF YOUR KINGDOM; THROUGH JESUS CHRIST OUR LORD.

PRAYER OF FRANCIS OF ASSISI

Lord, make me an instrument of your peace,
Where there is hatred, let me sow love;
Where there is injury, pardon;
Where there is doubt, faith;
Where there is despair, hope;
Where there is darkness, light;
Where there is sadness, joy;
O Divine Master,
grant that I may not so much seek to be consoled,
as to console;
to be understood, as to understand;
to be loved, as to love.
For it is in giving that we receive,
it is in pardoning that we are pardoned,
and it is in dying that we are born to eternal life.

PRAYER FOR THE WEEK

PRAYER FOR GRACE

Lord God, almighty and everlasting Father, you have brought us in safety to this new day. Preserve us with your mighty power, that we may not fall into sin, nor be overcome by adversity; and in all we do, direct us to the fulfilling of your purpose; through Jesus Christ our Lord.

PRAYER OF THANKSGIVING

Almighty God, Father of all mercies,
We your unworthy servants give you humble thanks
For all your goodness and loving-kindness
To us and all whom you have made.
We bless you for our creation, preservation,
And all the blessings of this life;
But above all for your immeasurable love
In the redemption of the world through our Lord Jesus Christ;
For the means of grace, and for the hope of glory.
And, we pray, give us such an awareness of your mercies,
That with truly thankful hearts we may show forth your praise,
Not only with our lips, but in our lives,
By giving up our selves to your service,
And by walking before you
In holiness and righteousness all our days;
Through Jesus Christ our Lord,
To whom, with you and the Holy Spirit,
Be honor and glory throughout all ages.
Amen.

DECLARATION OF VICTORY

CHRIST HAS DIED.
CHRIST IS RISEN.
CHRIST WILL COME AGAIN.

JESUS PRAYER

APPENDIX II
"PRAYER FOR THE WEEK" GUIDE

(Note: Each of these prayers come from the Book of Common Prayer. Depending on how the calendar falls, some prayers will be skipped. You can stay on track with the "Prayer for the Week" at www.healthyprayer.com)

Fourth Sunday before Christmas

Almighty God, give us grace to cast away the works of darkness, and put on the armor of light, now in the time of this mortal life in which your Son Jesus Christ came to visit us in great humility; that in the last day, when he shall come again in his glorious majesty to judge both the living and the dead, we may rise to the life immortal; through him who lives and reigns with you and the Holy Spirit, one God, now and for ever. Amen.

Third Sunday before Christmas

Merciful God, who sent your messengers the prophets to preach repentance and prepare the way for our salvation: Give us grace to heed their warnings and forsake our sins, that we may greet with joy the coming of Jesus Christ our Redeemer; who lives and reigns with you and the Holy Spirit, one God, now and for ever. Amen.

Second Sunday before Christmas

Stir up your power, O Lord, and with great might come among us; and, because we are sorely hindered by our sins, let your bountiful grace and mercy speedily help and deliver us; through Jesus Christ our Lord, to whom, with you and the Holy Spirit, be honor and glory, now and for ever. Amen.

The Sunday before Christmas

Purify our conscience, Almighty God, by your daily visitation, that your Son Jesus Christ, at his coming, may find in us a mansion prepared for himself; who lives and reigns with you, in the unity of the Holy Spirit, one God, now and for ever. Amen.

First Sunday after Christmas

Almighty God, you have poured upon us the new light of your incarnate Word: Grant that this light, enkindled in our hearts, may shine forth in our lives; through Jesus Christ our Lord, who lives and reigns with you, in the unity of the Holy Spirit, one God, now and for ever. Amen.

Second Sunday after Christmas Day

O God, who wonderfully created, and yet more wonderfully restored, the dignity of human nature: Grant that we may share the divine life of him who humbled himself to share our humanity, your Son Jesus Christ; who lives and reigns with you, in the unity of the Holy Spirit, one God, for ever and ever. Amen.

Sunday closest to January 6 (on the 6th or after)

Father in heaven, who at the baptism of Jesus in the River Jordan proclaimed him your beloved Son and anointed him with the Holy Spirit: Grant that all who are baptized into his Name may keep the covenant they have made, and boldly confess him as Lord and Savior; who with you and the Holy Spirit lives and reigns, one God, in glory everlasting. Amen.

Sunday closest to January 13

Almighty God, whose Son our Savior Jesus Christ is the light of the world: Grant that your people, illumined by your Word, may shine with the radiance of Christ's glory, that he may be known, worshiped, and obeyed to the ends of the earth; through Jesus Christ our Lord, who with you and the Holy Spirit lives and reigns, one God, now and for ever. Amen.

Sunday closest to January 20

Give us grace, O Lord, to answer readily the call of our Savior Jesus Christ and proclaim to all people the Good News of his salvation, that we and the whole world may perceive the glory of his marvelous works; who lives and reigns with you and the Holy Spirit, one God, for ever and ever. Amen.

Sunday closest to January 27

Almighty and everlasting God, you govern all things both in heaven and on earth: Mercifully hear the supplications of your people, and in our time grant us your peace; through Jesus Christ our Lord, who lives and reigns with you and the Holy Spirit, one God, for ever and ever. Amen.

Sunday closest to February 3

Set us free, O God, from the bondage of our sins, and give us the liberty of that abundant life which you have made known to us in your Son our Savior Jesus Christ; who lives and reigns with you, in the unity of the Holy Spirit, one God, now and for ever. Amen.

Sunday closest to February 10

O God, the strength of all who put their trust in you: Mercifully accept our prayers; and because in our weakness we can do nothing good without you, give us the help of your grace, that in keeping your commandments we may please you both in will and deed; through Jesus Christ our Lord, who lives and reigns with you and the Holy Spirit, one God, for ever and ever. Amen.

Sunday closest to February 17

O Lord, you have taught us that without love whatever we do is worth nothing; Send your Holy Spirit and pour into our hearts your greatest gift, which is love, the true bond of peace and of all virtue, without which whoever lives is accounted dead before you. Grant this for the sake of your only Son Jesus Christ, who lives and reigns with you and the Holy Spirit, one God, now and for ever. Amen.

Sunday closest to February 24

Most loving Father, whose will it is for us to give thanks for all things, to fear nothing but the loss of you, and to cast all our care on you who care for us: Preserve us from faithless fears and worldly anxieties, that no clouds of this mortal life may hide from us the light of that love which is immortal, and which you have manifested to us in your Son Jesus Christ our Lord; who lives and reigns with you, in the unity of the Holy Spirit, one God, now and for ever. Amen.

Sunday closest to March 3

O God, who before the passion of your only-begotten Son revealed his glory upon the holy mountain: Grant to us that we, beholding by faith the light of his countenance, may be strengthened to bear our cross, and be changed into his likeness from glory to glory; through Jesus Christ our Lord, who lives and reigns with you and the Holy Spirit, one God, for ever and ever. Amen.

Sixth Sunday before Easter

Almighty God, whose blessed Son was led by the Spirit to be tempted by Satan; Come quickly to help us who are assaulted by many temptations; and, as you know the weaknesses of each of us, let each one find you mighty to save; through Jesus Christ your Son our Lord, who lives and reigns with you and the Holy Spirit, one God, now and for ever. Amen.

Fifth Sunday before Easter

O God, whose glory it is always to have mercy: Be gracious to all who have gone astray from your ways, and bring them again with penitent hearts and steadfast faith to embrace and hold fast the unchangeable truth of your Word, Jesus Christ your Son; who with you and the Holy Spirit lives and reigns, one God, for ever and ever. Amen.

Fourth Sunday before Easter

Almighty God, you know that we have no power in ourselves to help ourselves: Keep us both outwardly in our bodies and inwardly in our souls, that we may be defended from all adversities which may happen to the body, and from all evil thoughts which may assault and hurt the soul; through Jesus Christ our Lord, who lives and reigns with you and the Holy Spirit, one God, for ever and ever. Amen.

Third Sunday before Easter

Gracious Father, whose blessed Son Jesus Christ came down from heaven to be the true bread which gives life to the world: Evermore give us this bread, that he may live in us, and we in him; who lives and reigns with you and the Holy Spirit, one God, now and for ever. Amen.

Second Sunday before Easter

Almighty God, you alone can bring into order the unruly wills and affections of sinners: Grant your people grace to love what you command and desire what you promise; that, among the swift and varied changes of the world, our hearts may surely there be fixed where true joys are to be found; through Jesus Christ our Lord, who lives and reigns with you and the Holy Spirit, one God, now and for ever. Amen.

Palm Sunday

Almighty and everliving God, in your tender love for the human race you sent your Son our Savior Jesus Christ to take upon him our nature, and to suffer death upon the cross, giving us the example of his great humility: Mercifully grant that we may walk in the way of his suffering, and also share in his resurrection; through Jesus Christ our Lord, who lives and reigns with you and the Holy Spirit, one God, for ever and ever. Amen

Easter Sunday

O God, who for our redemption gave your only-begotten Son to the death of the cross, and by his glorious resurrection delivered us from the power of our enemy: Grant us so to die daily to sin, that we may evermore live with him in the joy of his resurrection; through Jesus Christ your Son our Lord, who lives and reigns with you and the Holy Spirit, one God, now and for ever. Amen.

Or this

Almighty God, who through your only-begotten Son Jesus Christ overcame death and opened to us the gate of everlasting life: Grant that we, who celebrate with joy the day of the Lord's resurrection, may be raised from the death of sin by your life-giving Spirit; through Jesus Christ our Lord, who lives and reigns with you and the Holy Spirit, one God, now and for ever. Amen.

First Sunday after Easter

Almighty and everlasting God, who in the death and resurrection of Christ established the new covenant of reconciliation: Grant that all who have been reborn into the fellowship of Christ's Body may show forth in their lives what they profess by their faith; through Jesus Christ our Lord, who lives and reigns with you and the Holy Spirit, one God, for ever and ever. Amen.

Second Sunday after Easter

O God, whose blessed Son made himself known to his disciples in the breaking of bread: Open the eyes of our faith, that we may behold him in all his redeeming work; who lives and reigns with you, in the unity of the Holy Spirit, one God, now and for ever. Amen.

Third Sunday after Easter

O God, whose Son Jesus is the good shepherd of your people; Grant that when we hear his voice we may know him who calls us each by name, and follow where he leads; who, with you and the Holy Spirit, lives and reigns, one God, for ever and ever. Amen.

Fourth Sunday after Easter

Almighty God, whom truly to know is everlasting life: Grant us so perfectly to know your Son Jesus Christ to be the way, the truth, and the life, that we may steadfastly follow his steps in the way that leads to eternal life; through Jesus Christ your Son our Lord, who lives and reigns with you, in the unity of the Holy Spirit, one God, for ever and ever. Amen.

Fifth Sunday after Easter

O God, you have prepared for those who love you such good things as surpass our understanding: Pour into our hearts such love towards you, that we, loving you in all things and above all things, may obtain your promises, which exceed all that we can desire; through Jesus Christ our Lord, who lives and reigns with you and the Holy Spirit, one God, for ever and ever. Amen.

Sixth Sunday after Easter

O God, the King of glory, you have exalted your only Son Jesus Christ with great triumph to your kingdom in heaven: Do not leave us comfortless, but send us your Holy Spirit to strengthen us, and exalt us to that place where our Savior Christ has gone before; who lives and reigns with you and the Holy Spirit, one God, in glory everlasting. Amen.

Pentecost Sunday

Almighty God, on this day you opened the way of eternal life to every race and nation by the promised gift of your Holy Spirit: Shed abroad this gift throughout the world by the preaching of the Gospel, that it may reach to the ends of the earth; through Jesus Christ our Lord, who lives and reigns with you, in the unity of the Holy Spirit, one God, for ever and ever. Amen.

Or this

O God, who on this day taught the hearts of your faithful people by sending to them the light of your Holy Spirit: Grant us by the same Spirit to have a right judgment in all things, and evermore to rejoice in his holy comfort; through Jesus Christ your Son our Lord, who lives and reigns with you, in the unity of the Holy Spirit, one God, for ever and ever. Amen.

The Sunday after Pentecost Sunday

Almighty and everlasting God, you have given to us your servants grace, by the confession of a true faith, to acknowledge the glory of the eternal Trinity, and in the power of your divine Majesty to worship the Unity: Keep us steadfast in this faith and worship, and bring us at last to see you in your one and eternal glory, O Father; who with the Son and the Holy Spirit live and reign, one God, for ever and ever. Amen.

Sunday closest to May 11

Remember, O Lord, what you have wrought in us and not what we deserve; and, as you have called us to your service, make us worthy of our calling; through Jesus Christ our Lord, who lives and reigns with you and the Holy Spirit, one God, now and for ever. Amen.

Sunday closest to May 18

Almighty and merciful God, in your goodness keep us, we pray, from all things that may hurt us, that we, being ready both in mind and body, may accomplish with free hearts those things which belong to your purpose; through Jesus Christ our Lord, who lives and reigns with you and the Holy Spirit, one God, now and for ever. Amen.

Sunday closest to May 25

Grant, O Lord, that the course of this world may be peaceably governed by your providence; and that your Church may joyfully serve you in confidence and serenity; through Jesus Christ our Lord, who lives and reigns with you and the Holy Spirit, one God, for ever and ever. Amen.

Sunday closest to June 1

O God, your never-failing providence sets in order all things both in heaven and earth: Put away from us, we entreat you, all hurtful things, and give us those things which are profitable for us; through Jesus Christ our Lord, who lives and reigns with you and the Holy Spirit, one God, for ever and ever. Amen.

Sunday closest to June 8

O God, from whom all good proceeds: Grant that by your inspiration we may think those things that are right, and by your merciful guiding may do them; through Jesus Christ our Lord, who lives and reigns with you and the Holy Spirit, one God, for ever and ever. Amen.

Sunday closest to June 15

Keep, O Lord, your household the Church in your steadfast faith and love, that through your grace we may proclaim your truth with boldness, and minister your justice with compassion; for the sake of our Savior Jesus Christ, who lives and reigns with you and the Holy Spirit, one God, now and for ever. Amen.

Sunday closest to June 22

O Lord, make us have perpetual love and reverence for your holy Name, for you never fail to help and govern those whom you have set upon the sure foundation of your loving-kindness; through Jesus Christ our Lord, who lives and reigns with you and the Holy Spirit, one God, for ever and ever. Amen.

Sunday closest to June 29

Almighty God, you have built your Church upon the foundation of the apostles and prophets, Jesus Christ himself being the chief cornerstone: Grant us so to be joined together in unity of spirit by their teaching, that we may be made a holy temple acceptable to you; through Jesus Christ our Lord, who lives and reigns with you and the Holy Spirit, one God, for ever and ever. Amen.

Sunday closest to July 6

O God, you have taught us to keep all your commandments by loving you and our neighbor: Grant us the grace of your Holy Spirit, that we may be devoted to you with our whole heart, and united to one another with pure affection; through Jesus Christ our Lord, who lives and reigns with you and the Holy Spirit, one God, for ever and ever. Amen.

Sunday closest to July 13

O Lord, mercifully receive the prayers of your people who call upon you, and grant that they may know and understand what things they ought to do, and also may have grace and power faithfully to accomplish them; through Jesus Christ our Lord, who lives and reigns with you and the Holy Spirit, one God, now and for ever. Amen.

Sunday closest to July 20

Almighty God, the fountain of all wisdom, you know our necessities before we ask and our ignorance in asking: Have compassion on our weakness, and mercifully give us those things which for our unworthiness we dare not, and for our blindness we cannot ask; through the worthiness of your Son Jesus Christ our Lord, who lives and reigns with you and the Holy Spirit, one God, now and for ever. Amen.

Sunday closest to July 27

O God, the protector of all who trust in you, without whom nothing is strong, nothing is holy: Increase and multiply upon us your mercy; that, with you as our ruler and guide, we may so pass through things temporal, that we lose not the things eternal; through Jesus Christ our Lord, who lives and reigns with you and the Holy Spirit, one God, for ever and ever. Amen.

Sunday closest to August 3

Let your continual mercy, O Lord, cleanse and defend your Church; and, because it cannot continue in safety without your help, protect and govern it always by your goodness; through Jesus Christ our Lord, who lives and reigns with you and the Holy Spirit, one God, for ever and ever. Amen.

Sunday closest to August 10

Grant to us, Lord, we pray, the spirit to think and do always those things that are right, that we, who cannot exist without you, may by you be enabled to live according to your will; through Jesus Christ our Lord, who lives and reigns with you and the Holy Spirit, one God, for ever and ever. Amen.
Preface of the Lord's Day

Sunday closest to August 17

Almighty God, you have given your only Son to be for us a sacrifice for sin, and also an example of godly life: Give us grace to receive thankfully the fruits of this redeeming work, and to follow daily in the blessed steps of his most holy life; through Jesus Christ your Son our Lord, who lives and reigns with you and the Holy Spirit, one God, now and for ever. Amen.

Sunday closest to August 24

Grant, O merciful God, that your Church, being gathered together in unity by your Holy Spirit, may show forth your power among all peoples, to the glory of your Name; through Jesus Christ our Lord, who lives and reigns with you and the Holy Spirit, one God, for ever and ever. Amen. Preface of the Lord's Day

Sunday closest to August 31

Lord of all power and might, the author and giver of all good things: Graft in our hearts the love of your Name; increase in us true religion; nourish us with all goodness; and bring forth in us the fruit of good works; through Jesus Christ our Lord, who lives and reigns with you and the Holy Spirit, one God, for ever and ever. Amen.

Sunday closest to September 7

Grant us, O Lord, to trust in you with all our hearts; for, as you always resist the proud who confide in their own strength, so you never forsake those who make their boast of your mercy; through Jesus Christ our Lord, who lives and reigns with you and the Holy Spirit, one God, now and for ever. Amen.

Sunday closest to September 14

O God, because without you we are not able to please you, mercifully grant that your Holy Spirit may in all things direct and rule our hearts; through Jesus Christ our Lord, who lives and reigns with you and the Holy Spirit, one God, now and for ever. Amen.

Sunday closest to September 21

Grant us, Lord, not to be anxious about earthly things, but to love things heavenly; and even now, while we are placed among things that are passing away, to hold fast to those that shall endure; through Jesus Christ our Lord, who lives and reigns with you and the Holy Spirit, one God, for ever and ever. Amen.

Sunday closest to September 28

O God, you declare your almighty power chiefly in showing mercy and pity: Grant us the fullness of your grace, that we, running to obtain your promises, may become partakers of your heavenly treasure; through Jesus Christ our Lord, who lives and reigns with you and the Holy Spirit, one God, for ever and ever. Amen.

Sunday closest to October 5

Almighty and everlasting God, you are always more ready to hear than we to pray, and to give more than we either desire or deserve: Pour upon us the abundance of your mercy, forgiving us those things of which our conscience is afraid, and giving us those good things for which we are not worthy to ask, except through the merits and mediation of Jesus Christ our Savior; who lives and reigns with you and the Holy Spirit, one God, for ever and ever. Amen.

Sunday closest to October 12

Lord, we pray that your grace may always precede and follow us, that we may continually be given to good works; through Jesus Christ our Lord, who lives and reigns with you and the Holy Spirit, one God, now and for ever. Amen.

Sunday closest to October 19

Almighty and everlasting God, in Christ you have revealed your glory among the nations: Preserve the works of your mercy, that your Church throughout the world may persevere with steadfast faith in the confession of your Name; through Jesus Christ our Lord, who lives and reigns with you and the Holy Spirit, one God, for ever and ever. Amen.

Sunday closest to October 26

Almighty and everlasting God, increase in us the gifts of faith, hope, and charity; and, that we may obtain what you promise, make us love what you command; through Jesus Christ our Lord, who lives and reigns with you and the Holy Spirit, one God, for ever and ever. Amen.

Sunday closest to November 2

Almighty and merciful God, it is only by your gift that your faithful people offer you true and laudable service: Grant that we may run without stumbling to obtain your heavenly promises; through Jesus Christ our Lord, who lives and reigns with you and the Holy Spirit, one God, now and for ever. Amen.

Sunday closest to November 9

O God, whose blessed Son came into the world that he might destroy the works of the devil and make us children of God and heirs of eternal life: Grant that, having this hope, we may purify ourselves as he is pure; that, when he comes again with power and great glory, we may be made like him in his eternal and glorious kingdom; where he lives and reigns with you and the Holy Spirit, one God, for ever and ever. Amen.

Sunday closest to November 16

Blessed Lord, who caused all holy Scriptures to be written for our learning: Grant us so to hear them, read, mark, learn, and inwardly digest them, that we may embrace and ever hold fast the blessed hope of everlasting life, which you have given us in our Savior Jesus Christ; who lives and reigns with you and the Holy Spirit, one God, for ever and ever. Amen.

Sunday closest to November 23

Almighty and everlasting God, whose will it is to restore all things in your well-beloved Son, the King of kings and Lord of lords: Mercifully grant that the peoples of the earth, divided and enslaved by sin, may be freed and brought together under his most gracious rule; who lives and reigns with you and the Holy Spirit, one God, now and for ever. Amen.

APPENDIX III
THE LORD'S PRAYER AS A TRELLIS

Some readers may be familiar with the concept of using the Lord's Prayer as an outline for prayer. This is something I often practice when I lead corporate prayer gatherings. I find it to be especially helpful in group settings; however, it can also provide a wonderful approach to personal prayer.

Below is an example of how to use the Lord's Prayer as a "trellis," incorporating each element discussed throughout this book: structure, silence, and spontaneity.

PRAISE

OUR FATHER, WHO ART IN HEAVEN,
HALLOWED BE THY NAME.

- Spend a few moments recognizing God for who he is.
- Praise him as our Father who loves us passionately and unconditionally.
- Praise him for his holiness, his faithfulness, his goodness, etc.

AGENDA

THY KINGDOM COME,
THY WILL BE DONE
ON EARTH AS IT IS IN HEAVEN.

- Pray for God's will to be done in whatever pressing situations exist in your mind.
- Pray for God's will to be done in your marriage and family.
- Pray for governmental leadership (local, state, national, and worldwide).
- Pray for the faithfulness of churches.
- Pray for the advancement of God's kingdom on earth.
- Pray for missionaries and church leaders.
- Pray for justice and peace on earth.
- Pray for people you know personally who need to welcome Jesus and his reign into their lives.

PROVISION

GIVE US THIS DAY OUR DAILY BREAD.

- Thank God for his provision in your life (spiritually, mentally, emotionally, and physically).
- Ask God to provide the "spiritual bread" you need today.
- Pray for those who are struggling with health or other personal issues.
- Pray for those around the world who lack basic essentials.
- In asking, be open to the possibility of God calling upon you to help provide for the daily needs of others.

FORGIVENESS

*AND FORGIVE US OUR TRESPASSES,
AS WE FORGIVE THOSE WHO TRESPASS AGAINST US.*

- Examine your life and ask God to wash you of sinful actions, words, attitudes, and motives.
- Thank God for the forgiveness he provides

through the cross and resurrection of Jesus Christ.
- Pray for those who have sinned against you. Forgive them and ask God to forgive them.
- Pray for those who have declared themselves to be your enemies—whether personal enemies or national enemies.

PROTECTION

AND LEAD US NOT INTO TEMPTATION, BUT DELIVER US FROM EVIL.

- Ask God to help those who are experiencing spiritual trials.
- Pray for protection from the tactics of the enemy.
- Pray for the safety of those who are in hotspots around the world (wars, earthquakes, famines, etc.).
- Ask God to protect and sustain the faith of fellow Christians who are experiencing persecution in various places around the world.

DOXOLOGY

FOR THINE IS THE KINGDOM AND THE POWER AND THE GLORY FOREVER.
AMEN.

- Spend a few moments in silent prayer before the Lord.
- Seal your time with God with a word of praise.

ACKNOWLEDGEMENTS

I wish to thank my wonderful wife, Carrie, for her unwavering support and assistance throughout the making of this book. I am such a blessed man to have her as my partner on this journey.

I am so grateful for the ministry of Brian Zahnd, pastor of Word of Life Church in St. Joseph, Missouri. While I have gleaned from many authors and speakers over the years, his weekend prayer school served as the main catalyst for my own transformation in prayer.

Thanks to Ellen Edelman for her hard work and helpful suggestions. She has been a dedicated, patient, and thorough editor.

I also would like to thank Woody Gunnels for his valuable input.